PIZZA! PIZZA! PIZZA!

PIZZA! PIZZA! PIZZA!

Over 75 Fresh Ideas for Every Pizza Night

Sara Haas

hatherleigh

Hatherleigh Press is committed to preserving and protecting the natural resources of the earth. Environmentally responsible and sustainable practices are embraced within the company's mission statement.

Visit us at www.hatherleighpress.com.

Pizza! Pizza! Pizza!

Library of Congress Cataloging-in-Publication Data

is available upon request.

ISBN: 978-1-57826-968-6

COVER AND INTERIOR DESIGN BY CAROLYN KASPER

PHOTOGRAPHY BY SARA HAAS

ILLUSTRATION ON PAGE 192 © EMILY HAAS

Printed in the United States

10 9 8 7 6 5 4 3 2 1

For my loving and patient husband,
my adorable sous chef, and my beyond
supportive friends, family, and colleagues.
And for our little Lucy, you will always
be in our hearts.

Contents

HELLO & WELCOME IX

PIZZA BASICS: THE INGREDIENTS 1

PIZZA BASICS: TOOLS & TIPS 13

READING THE RECIPES 21

DOUGH & CRUSTS 33

SAUCES 43

VEGETARIAN PIZZA 65

SPECIALTY PIZZA 119

SALADS & SALAD-STYLE PIZZA 145

DESSERT PIZZA 165

PERFECT PIZZA EXTRAS 173

BONUS STUFF 179

RECIPE INDEX 191

Hello & Welcome

L ET ME START BY saying one thing—this *isn't* your average pizza cookbook. First of all, I'm a registered dietitian with a culinary degree, so that automatically makes this cookbook different from any of the other pizza cookbooks out there! But even though I love nutrition, this book isn't a lecture on nutrients and calories. Instead, once you dig in, you'll find out what I discovered a long time ago—that pizza can absolutely be a nourishing food for both the stomach *and* the mind. You read that right. Pizza checks all of the boxes when it comes to flavor, satisfaction and yes, even nutrition!

I've designed this book as a resource for pizza making, but not in the traditional way. I didn't travel to Italy to learn about hand-crafted pizza ovens, artisan flour and sun-soaked Italian tomatoes (although I would love to someday!) and I didn't work under any master pizza makers to learn their skills (although I'd love to do that, too). Instead, I learned by teaching myself. Does that make me an expert? Heck, no! But I know what I like, and I like pizza, so I did the research and I've been spending years perfecting my own technique, right in my little Chicago apartment kitchen. And I want to share it all with you, the home cook. I like to think of this cookbook as a "pizza experience"—one that's approachable and fun, like me!

SOME BACKSTORY

As a kid, I loved pizza. Most kids do, right? My favorite came from a small local chain in Indianapolis, Indiana called Noble Romans. You could watch them make the pizza through a window, which, at the tender age of 8, I thought was super cool. (And FYI, I still thought it was cool around 12 because those 16-year-old boys tossing the pizza in the air were pretty darn cute.) The hand-tossed cheese pizza at Noble Romans was my favorite, followed by their breadsticks and cheese sauce. We made my mom get two orders of those and we ate them warm, right out of the bag on the way home.

I can even remember one time when my mom made the bad (unbeknownst to her) choice of dining in and my brother (by the way, he's two years older than me, which is relevant to the story because he's the one who should be responsible and setting a good example, right?) almost set the place on fire. Apparently, he felt the need to test the theory that paper napkins will burn if placed directly over the flame of a candle. Spoiler alert, they do! Somehow my mom contained the fire and I'm pretty sure Noble Romans removed candles from the table after that.

Fast forward to high school, I needed a job. You know, to buy scrunchies, hoop earrings and oversized sweaters...hey, it was the 90s! Luckily, I had an "in" at a local, gourmet-ish pizza place. I say "gourmet-ish" because at the time, Indianapolis didn't really have pizza restaurants, let alone one that had *gasp* fresh tomatoes as a topping! So fancy! My friend worked there and she helped me get a job there, too. I started out answering the phones. Have you ever had a job answering phones? It's torture. Imagine answering the phone the same way fifty times a day— "Hello, this is Indy Pizza, what would you like to order?" And if we were busy, "Hello, this is Indy Pizza, can you hold please?" And then you've got seven people on hold and you're trying to remember who called first! All of those flashing phone lines, ahh!

Then there was their order. The phone was located in the kitchen, so it was impossible to hear. Most people spoke way too fast and way too quiet. And oh yeah, this was *before* computers, so I had to write the orders on a piece of paper to hand-deliver to the guys making pizza. Since time was of the essence, I also had to learn all of the shorthand for

the ingredients and the specialty pizzas we had. Oh, and did I mention that I also made all of the salads, for both the carry-out and the restaurant? It was madness. Plus, I had to be nice. Who can be nice while doing all of that?

When my boss asked me if I wanted to switch to kitchen prep, I jumped at the opportunity! YES! No more answering phones! Hallelujah! So, I started coming to work in the late morning and joined the prep crew and I *loved* it. No one really talked (it was glorious), we just prepped all of the ingredients for the evening slam. The music would be blasting (lots of Johnny Cash, The Grateful Dead, Pink Floyd and Phish) and we'd all just be bobbing our heads as we made salad dressing, chopped lettuce, prepared dough, and shredded cheese. It was my first taste of the magic of the kitchen.

In college, while earning my nutrition degree, I worked at a restaurant as well. But this was a "fine dining" establishment. My job was to make salads, appetizers and desserts. I liked it, but besides the sous chef who was extremely quirky, the place was full of stuffy staff and patrons. I missed my pizza friends—the music, the joking around, the *fun.* I needed the job though and it paid decently, so I stayed.

After college, I moved to Chicago and, you guessed it, I needed a job, so I worked in *another* restaurant. This time I was at the front of the house and worked as a hostess and then a waitress. I hated it. I mean, I loved the people I worked with, but man, the people who came to eat at the restaurant really sucked. I've always half-jokingly said that everyone should at one point in their life work as a waiter/waitress because it teaches you about being a better human. I can't tell you the number of times I was treated like a brainless robot. I almost quit at least a hundred times. Luckily, my degree in nutrition finally landed me a job working as a dietitian at a local hospital.

I was so pumped to start my "career" and happy that I finally had a "real" job. "Look mom and dad, all of that college is finally paying off!" But guess what? I hated it. Yep, every

part of it. I didn't like being in the hospital. I didn't like sick people. And I didn't like all of the doctors who seemed to think my job wasn't as important as theirs. I started wondering what the heck I was doing. None of it was great and I couldn't wait to get out of there, but I didn't know where to go. I needed a change and luckily found a job working as a consultant dietitian. I loved the company and my boss (love you Maggie Roche!), but it was a hard job. I had to be available to travel (sometimes over an hour drive each way) and be prepared to cover a variety of roles. That meant I had to be confident, no matter the situation.

It was during all of my long drives to different hospitals, nursing homes and other places full of sick people that I began to daydream about culinary school. I had always loved food, but I started to wonder if it was possible to turn my love into a career. After plenty of discussions with many people, I finally made the decision. I was going to do it. I continued working as a dietitian but spent my mornings in classes at a local culinary school. It made for some long, tiring days, but I knew (most of the time) it would be worth it.

One of the best parts of culinary school was learning about bread and dough (maybe I should have gone to Baking & Pastry school instead). I had two excellent instructors who were passionate about it and their excitement was contagious. I can still remember one of the instructors telling us to lean in and listen while our dough was kneading in the stand mixer. He wanted us to hear the "angel wings" flapping (the dough starting to build structure and lightly slap the sides of the bowl), so that we'd know when the dough had been kneaded enough. Oh, the smile and joy on his face is such a lasting memory! That love is why their words still stick with me to this day!

One particular instructor (Chef Tom, I'm talking about you!) held "Bread Guild" once a month on a weekend. He would come in on his off day to bake bread with us. It was such a cool experience and I loved that he did this for us. I listened and learned and asked a lot of questions. Eventually, I began to understand how nuanced making bread actually is. Why a scale (measuring in weight) was crucial, the differences between yeasts, how to know when your dough was over-proofed—there was so much to know! I found it fascinating.

I took all of that information and started playing at home. With bread, of course, but also with pizza dough. I wanted to make it at home, and I wanted it to taste just as good, if not better, than the stuff you order at a restaurant. I can't tell you how many videos I watched and how much research I did about how to make pizza—and this was *before* YouTube. I figured out how to get my home oven to work for me, why a pizza stone was so important, and how to get that pesky dough shaped into a circle. Again, I loved it. After plenty of experimentation, I finally figured a few things out, including a good dough recipe. Then I was off. Hundreds of pizzas later, I'm here, writing this book. Not because I'm an expert in all things pizza, but because I just love it so much.

I know that I could've never written this book without all of those life experiences. All of my successes, all of my failures, and everything in between, have led me to this point. And even if I only sell one single book, I don't care, because I've been given the chance to share my love of pizza with YOU! And it feels so good! So sit back, relax and read on!

BUT WHAT ABOUT NUTRITION?

Wait! You care about nutrition? ME TOO! In fact, I care about it so much that I went to school to learn all about it. And I took it so far that I even got a degree in it. *But* . . . sometimes nutrition becomes a roadblock for people. They're either obsessed with it or completely turned off by it. And I get both opinions. So while, yes, I am a dietitian, I'm also a person living in the real world. And I know that good health and nutrition are important, but being consumed by it is not. That's why my stance is, and forever will be, eat the foods that make you feel good and don't overdo it.

You'll soon notice a recurring theme in this cookbook, and that theme is: *eat more plants*! Why? Plants are delicious! Is there anything better than a juicy tomato or a bunch of fresh herbs? The answer is "no!"

Second, consuming more plant-based foods is a great way of helping Mother Nature. Plants require less water and fewer other natural resources to grow than animals grown for food. Plus, plant scraps can be composted and returned to the earth to grow, you guessed it, more plants!

Lastly, plants are nutritious! If you're a health-conscious person, which I interpret as someone who wants to consume foods that make them feel good, you hopefully know that plants supply an amazing array of nutrients that support health and prevent disease. For all of these reasons, plants are on and in every single pizza in this cookbook.

Even the dough!

You heard that right. While there are certainly recipes in this collection that don't use whole grain flour, all my favorite ones do. I love the extra fiber and B vitamins it provides, but even more importantly, whole wheat flour tastes *good*. It adds a sweet, nutty flavor and provides a bit of "chew" to the dough. It's lovely and I'm 99 percent sure you'll agree once you try it.

Without any further ado, let's get you started on the basics of perfect pizza preparation and before you know it, you'll be in your very own kitchen making the best pizza you've ever tasted!

PIZZA BASICS: THE INGREDIENTS

ANY CHEF WILL TELL you that to create delicious food, you need good ingredients. I'm sure, however, we can all agree that a fast food hotdog or a frozen pizza can be pretty darn tasty. But for the most part, yes, good ingredients are crucial. And "good ingredients" don't equate to the most expensive ingredients. It's about choosing quality and freshness, reliable brands and food that makes you feel good. So, just keep that in mind when you're choosing what you put on your pizza. That $1 pepperoni is going to taste like $1 pepperoni. It's up to you!

THE DOUGH

Flour

If you've been to the grocery store, you've likely seen the vast array of flours available. If I didn't know better, I would say almost anything can be turned into flour—chickpeas, cassava, the list goes on and on. Those alternative flours are all fine and good, but from my experience (as a healthy individual without any food intolerances or allergies), wheat flour makes the best pizza. Yes, this is my opinion, but there's a bit of science to back it up.

All wheat flour is made from wheat berries (or kernels). Wheat is a grain composed of three parts: the bran (B vitamins, fiber and minerals), the germ (healthy fats, antioxidants, vitamin E and B vitamins) and the endosperm (mostly carbohydrates with a smattering of protein and vitamins). The milling process separates these components from each other. To create all-purpose flour, only the starchy endosperm is used and milled into flour. Whole wheat flour, on the other hand, includes all three components, which means it has more protein than all-purpose flour and more nutrition.

Most wheat flour comes from hard and soft wheat varieties; the difference between the two is their protein content. Hard wheat has a higher protein content than soft wheat. This is important because the proteins in wheat are what give pizza dough its elasticity, structure and texture, and why hard wheat is favored for bread and pizza making.

There are two proteins in wheat, gliadin and glutenin, and when they're introduced to water and kneading, they bond together to form a network of long strands (gluten). This network is comparable to the human skeleton. Just like your skeleton supports the structure of your body, gluten stabilizes and supports the structure of the dough. It traps the gases formed during the fermentation process, which allows the dough to rise. It also ensures the pizza doesn't collapse while it's baking. It makes sense then, that dough without the development of that gluten structure, will result in a flat and dense pizza.

Knowing all of this, it should be easy to pick the best flour for pizza dough...right? Yes, kind of. There's more to pizza than flour, but to achieve the highest level of success, I would recommend a combination of all-purpose flour (which is a mixture of hard and soft wheat and supplies 10–12 percent protein) and whole wheat flour (around 14–15 percent protein). I use this combination in my "50/50" dough recipe.

If you're not making the 50/50 dough, then I recommend using either bread flour or a combination of bread flour and all-purpose flour to create your dough. How do you choose? It comes down to preference. Using only all-purpose flour will produce a crispy crust but can also tear more easily (thanks to its lower gluten content) and using only bread flour (which is 12–13 percent protein) will produce a chewy crust and is a bit easier to shape and stretch than a completely all-purpose flour dough. You can use either in my recipes or a combination of the two.

The "00" Italian flours are nice, but because of their unique characteristics, are better suited for Neapolitan-style pizzas—where a super-hot oven (over 700°F!) is needed.

Water

Water is the second biggest ingredient in pizza dough recipes. It's pretty important too. Without water, it would be impossible to make pizza dough (remember, you just learned that when you were reading about flour). Its purpose is to hydrate the flour to develop the gluten and the ratio of water to flour matters!

Everything I'm going to tell you in this section is a bit more than you probably need to know, but it's fun to understand the science in case you need to fix a problem. So here we go!

You need water to hydrate the flour—hydration, in pizza terms, is the ratio of water to flour. Your pizza dough needs to be properly hydrated so that it can achieve its end goal of becoming a pizza. Most pizza recipes developed for the home cook are around 65–68 percent hydration. This creates a dough that is easy to work with, no matter your skill level. A lower hydration level works better for pizzas that only need a short amount of time in the oven—think commercial pizza ovens that can reach high temperatures. They don't require as much hydration because they only spend a short amount of time (maybe 2 or 3 minutes) in the oven. But home ovens can only get to around 500–550°F, so they need more time in the oven, which means they need a bit more hydration. That makes sense, right?

The recipes in this book are all around that 65–68 percent hydration level because they're all designed for the home cook who doesn't have a commercial oven.

Here's the deal, though: *other* things can get in the way of properly hydrating your dough. Maybe you didn't measure ingredients accurately, maybe the weather's too humid, maybe you live at high elevation. What can you do about these?

The first one is easy to tackle: use a food scale to measure your ingredients. Not only does this improve accuracy, but it's also actually much easier because you weigh everything in one bowl—which means fewer dishes. Kitchen scales can be found at all price points and even the least expensive option is a good one. Take care of it and it will last you a long time.

On to humidity. This one can be tricky, but the more you make pizza dough, the easier it will be to understand if your dough is properly hydrated. Humidity equals moisture. So, if you're making your pizza on a day when the humidity is high, you may need less water to hydrate your dough. If it's, say, a dry winter day and the humidity is low, then you may need a little extra water to hydrate the dough. Use the weather a bit to guide you.

Finally, elevation. If you live at higher altitudes, you may find that you'll need to add a bit more water. Flour seems to require more hydration with the increase in elevation. Adjust accordingly.

Salt

I use kosher salt in all of my pizza dough recipes. I like the larger crystals compared to the smaller, finer crystals of table salt. But honestly, any type of salt will work here. I like to add a decent amount of salt to my dough, but if you find it's too much, no worries, just back off a little until you get the amount you like.

Yeast

For the sake of ease, in this cookbook I only use active dry yeast or instant yeast. Both are readily available and both work well with my wheat-based and gluten-free flour doughs. What's the difference? Great question! First, it's important to know that yeast is *alive!* Cool, right? You can buy fresh yeast in the refrigerated section of the grocery store, but it has a short lifespan, 3–4 months once open, so it's not always a practical choice. You'll also need more of it (usually 3 times) than if you use active dry or instant yeast.

Active dry yeast is basically dehydrated yeast. Dehydrating the yeast causes it to go dormant. This means you have to re-hydrate it to bring it to life. To do that is simple, you combine the yeast with some warm water and optionally, a bit of sweetener (I use honey in this book, but granulated sugar is a fine substitute especially if preparing vegan). You let it sit for about 5 minutes and ta-da, you've got active yeast! How do you know it's come back to life? It should look foamy and bubbly. If it doesn't look like a tiny bubbling cauldron, well, that stinks because it means your yeast might not be good anymore. So, test another batch (you can follow package instructions too) and if it doesn't work, toss it and grab yourself some more from the store.

Instant yeast is also a dehydrated form of yeast, but it's manufactured so that it can be used without rehydrating. That means you can add it right along with the other ingredients and it will do its thing. This saves you time since you won't have to fuss with that water and foaming business.

I personally like active dry yeast because it confirms that it is still fresh and good to use, but the choice is totally up to you. Both work well and I've certainly had success with each. And in other great news, both active dry and instant can be bought in bulk (skip those packets which cost more!) and once opened, can be refrigerated for up to four months. Just keep it in a tightly sealed container towards the back of your fridge.

Sweeteners

Classic Neapolitan pizza dough recipes don't call for any sweetener. I love the simplicity, *but* from my experience, a little sweetness (honey, in my case, but sugar or agave extract works if you'd like to make the recipe vegan) to help feed the yeast is a good thing for most of the doughs in this book. Not only does sugar get the yeast "going," but it also adds some color to the cooked crust. A little bit is all you need, remember, we're not making cinnamon rolls! Too much sugar will interfere with gluten development, so stick to no more than one to two tablespoons.

Oil

I tend to use oil when I'm using whole wheat flour in my dough recipes. The oil helps when the time comes to stretch the dough. The result is a more pliable dough. That's a good thing, especially if you're new to dough-making. There's nothing worse than stretching your dough and having it tear. Oil helps with that while adding tenderness and a bit of flavor.

SAUCES

The type of sauce you use matters. Think of it like picking out a rug for your house...hear me out. When you pick out a rug, it's usually not an impulse buy. You've likely decided where you need it and how big it should be. The rug also has to make sense for the space; it should have the right pile, work with the furniture in the room and it should be a certain color. The rug helps pull the whole "look" of the room together, anchoring it. Sauce is like that rug. It's the ingredient that unifies all of the ingredients on the pizza. The wrong rug can ruin the vibe just like the wrong sauce can ruin the pizza. To complicate things, the sauce is also a matter of taste and preference. Just because I like the rug in that room or that sauce on that pizza, doesn't mean you will. Experiment a bit and have fun.

CHEESES

The cheese shop is one of my favorite places. There's nothing like having the cheesemonger slice off a piece of something magical for you to try. While I love artisan cheeses, they can be a bit pricey. But here's the good news—expensive cheese isn't usually the cheese you want for pizza. Save those high-end cheeses for your cheeseboard. Instead, find a good mozzarella that you (and your family) like. Use that as your go-to. Then experiment with other cheeses to accent that mozzarella, keeping in mind that the $50 feta isn't probably what you need.

Some pizzas can even be enjoyed *without* any cheese. While a traditional pizza (to most of us) isn't a pizza without cheese, sometimes the toppings are so good that cheese would mess with that. Speaking of no cheese: Many of the recipes, especially those in the Vegetarian section, can be made vegan by substituting your favorite vegan cheese equivalents and swapping out the honey in the dough for another vegan-friendly sweetener. Remember, this isn't a traditional pizza cookbook. So, I do a lot of stuff that isn't traditional. If that's not your thing, then throw some cheese on it—don't worry, we can still be friends!

TOPPINGS

Your pizza is as good as the ingredients you put on it. But again, it's all about *your* preferences. I will say though, there are some things that I swear by, like good quality canned tomatoes, fresh herbs and vegetables. Other than those things, I'm open for anything—canned, jarred, frozen, fresh—it all works and is worth trying. Again, experiment and have fun!

GENERAL INGREDIENTS

Black Pepper

I like freshly cracked. Call me a pepper snob, but I just think it's 100,000 percent better than the stuff that's already pulverized for you. But hey, if that's all you've got, it's better than nothing. Maybe.

Kosher Salt

This is the salt I use primarily throughout this book. I like it for its coarser texture and how evenly I can sprinkle it over stuff. Save the table salt for well, the table, and use those other fancy salts (pink Himalayan, platypus-foraged, sea salt) you got for your birthday as finishing salts (the stuff you add at the end to show off your elegance).

Extra-Virgin Olive Oil

Olive oil is my friend in the kitchen. I use it in the doughs in this book and many of the other recipes too. But if you run out for some reason, no worries! Many other neutral oils will work just fine. My other personal favorites are avocado oil, grapeseed oil and canola oil.

Citrus Juices

Whenever I mention citrus juice in this book, I mean fresh juice—it just tastes better. But since I know you may not always have access to fresh citrus juices, feel free to substitute with a bottled variety if necessary.

Citrus Zest

Before you even think of juicing any citrus, remove its zest first! If you're not using it immediately, place it on a damp paper towel and then in a resealable, zip-top bag and use within three days if refrigerated, and up to 1 month if frozen.

Fresh Herbs

To me, there's nothing more lovely than fresh herbs. They can elevate any dish. For herbs with soft stems such as cilantro and parsley, use the stems! They're just as flavorful. When I call for fresh herbs in this book, try and follow my lead. Because dried basil is fine, but fresh basil is excellent!

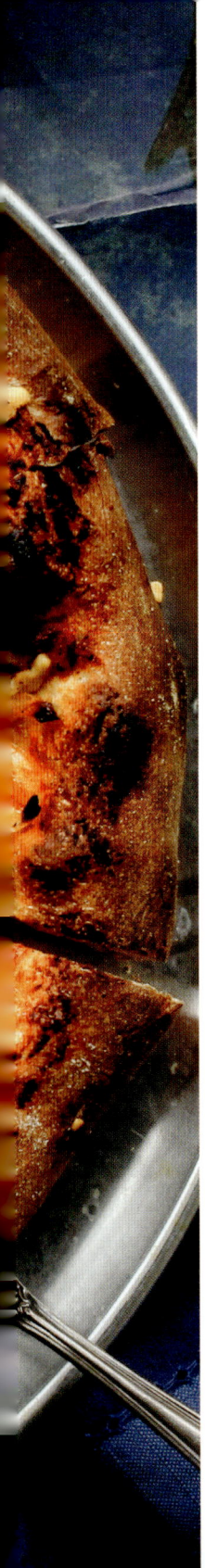

PIZZA BASICS: TOOLS & TIPS

I WISH I COULD SAY that you don't need any special tools to make pizza, and I suppose I could, but I don't think that's entirely true. Yes, you could make pizza without any of the items I list below, but you'll have more fun and be more successful if you have them. Hopefully you already have a few of these, but if not, go ahead and treat yourself. If you plan on making lots of pizza, which I hope you do, then consider this a good investment.

MY TOP TOOLS

Pizza Stone or Steel

If you're cooking in a conventional, home oven (which you likely are) I highly suggest getting a pizza stone or steel. That's why it's at the top of my list. As I discussed earlier, a home oven can't reach the same high temperatures as a commercial pizza oven. The stone and steel help retain and boost the heat of your oven. And they work. I have a stone and steel and I use them both.

So how do you choose? Honestly, just pick one or get both. I typically position my pizza stone on the second to lowest rack in my oven and the steel on the uppermost rack and I get great results with both. But all ovens are different, so experiment with rack placement and see what works best for your oven.

See below for more of an explanation on these two tools.

Pizza Stone

Material: Typically made from ceramic, cordierite stone or clay

Price: About $30

Heat conduction: Good

Heat retention: Good

Durability: Decent, but can crack or break easily and, if immediately introduced to high temperatures (thermal shock), will shatter

Pizza Steel

Material: Steel

Price: About $100

Heat conduction: Great (steel is a good conductor of heat)

Heat retention: Great

Durability: Great; not affected by thermal shock, so no worrying about shattering or breaking

---

TIPS FOR USING THE PIZZA STONE OR STEEL

I get plenty of questions about equipment. When it comes to pizza, I personally love both my baking stone and baking steel. But if I could choose only one, it would be the steel. Why? Because it helps turn your conventional home oven into a smoking hot pizzeria-style oven. Why wouldn't you want that?

Now that I've convinced you to make the investment, I wanted to share tips from Andris Lagsdin, inventor of the Baking Steel, about using and caring for it:

- **Most manufacturers recommend that you place the stone on the bottom rack of the oven or even on the floor of the oven while it preheats.** I say, experiment! My oven runs a bit hot, so I actually prefer my stone on the second to bottom rack and have good success.

- **The baking steel works great on the top rack for pizza.** You can even preheat the oven with it there. The great thing about the steel in this position is that once you've got a good bake on your pizza, you can switch to broil to "finish" the crust. This will produce a pie that mimics your favorite restaurant pizza! Alternatively, skip the broil and bake the pizza on the top rack for about 7 minutes.

- **Keep your steel in the oven.** Andris says storing it there has benefits, too. Your steel will regulate oven temperature for everything else you cook in there. A regulated temperature improves cooking, providing consistent heat.

- **Clean your stone or steel following the manufacturer's instructions.** I know, cleaning isn't my favorite part of cooking either, but it has to be done. You *can* put off cleaning your steel until the next day, just be sure to use a bench scraper or cleaning brick (made with recycled glass) to remove any stuck on bits. Then, use soap and water to clean, and pat it dry using a clean tea towel or paper towels. Before storing, wipe the surface with a thin layer of oil (Andris recommends canola or avocado).

Pizza Peel

I only invested in a pizza peel a few years ago, but I'm so glad I did. I have a short-handled, wooden version and I adore it. While not a necessity, it really makes transferring the pizza in and out of the oven much easier. They're not an expensive investment, so go for it. You'll most commonly find wooden or metal pizza peels. Wooden peels can be a bit thicker, which makes transferring the pizza into the oven easy. But that thickness can pose a challenge when removing pizza. I typically use parchment paper, though, so I'm able to pull a corner of parchment which helps me get my wooden peel underneath it. The choice is ultimately up to you.

Parchment Paper

I have a love affair with parchment paper. It's one of my favorite kitchen tools. It's so versatile and makes cooking and clean-up super easy. I use it in this book to build all of my pizzas. Yes, you can build your pizza directly on your pizza peel, but I prefer to make mine on a sheet of parchment, then transfer it to the peel. That way, I don't have to worry about sliding the pizza from the peel to the oven, which can be hard if you've put too many toppings on your pizza or you're a klutz like me.

Semolina or Fine Cornmeal

Some people think you have to choose one or the other. Not me! I say go with what works for you. I use either or both along with all-purpose flour to coat my peel or parchment before building my crust on it. The coarse texture acts like ball bearings, helping the pizza slide easier, which is great if you're using the pizza peel. I also like to use it for the texture it provides! There's something special about having that little bit of texture on the bottom of each pizza slice!

Stand Mixer

The stand mixer is another work horse in my kitchen. I make a *lot* of baked goods and cookies, and I don't know where I'd be without this thing. My parents gave it to me as a birthday present when I turned 23 and I still use it today, almost 20 years later! Stand mixers, when fitted with the dough hook attachment, are also great for making pizza dough. They do all of the hard work for you!

Bench Scraper

A bench scraper is a fun tool to have in the kitchen too. I like it as a way to divide the dough, as well as a tool to pick up the dough. You can also use it to clean all of that flour off your kitchen counter. Do you need it? No, but they're inexpensive and a nice tool for baking in general.

Pastry Scraper (Flexible)

A pastry scraper is similar to a bench scraper, but it's flexible. This one for me is a must have. I use the same one I got when I was in culinary school! I love it because it makes scooping dough out of the stand mixer super easy. I definitely recommend this type of scraper if you're going to be using the stand mixer to make your dough.

Blender or Food Processor

If you don't have one of these two, *please* get one. You can find them used or grab an inexpensive one that has good ratings. They're wonderful for making sauces, dips and salad dressings. I use mine all of the time. Larger sizes work best for dough, so take that into consideration before buying.

Pizza Wheel

Please, please get yourself a pizza wheel! Yes, a knife or scissors can also be used, but come on, a pizza wheel is so fun and so easy to use.

GENERAL STORAGE & FREEZING TIPS

Here's some great news about pizza dough: it stores *really* well. So if you run out of time to make it or if you want to make a big batch, no problem. Pizza dough can be kept in the refrigerator for about 72 hours. Place it in a container that's two times larger than the dough and has a lid or cover that can create a proper seal. I have a food storage container with a lid that I like to use. But in a pinch, I've used plastic lettuce containers (clamshells) and old takeout containers.

If that wasn't good enough news, you can also freeze pizza dough. Magnificent, right? My preferred method for this is to transfer the dough to a resealable plastic or silicone bag. I'll shape the dough into balls and then place one ball of dough in a bag. Then, I'll seal and label it and put it in the freezer. I recommend using it within six months. Before freezing, let it rise at least once. When you're ready to bake, allow it to fully thaw and go through another rise before using.

REHEATING TIPS

If you have leftover pizza, don't use the microwave to reheat it. You'll just end up with soggy, droopy pizza. Instead, I have two methods that I like to employ when I'm re-heating my pie. One of my favorite methods is on the stovetop. Place your pizza in a large skillet, try not to over-crowd it, and cover it with foil. Set it over a medium-low heat and let it go until the cheese is nice and melty. Check on it occasionally as you may need to adjust the heat a bit as your skillet warms up.

The second method uses the oven. Place a baking sheet in the oven and preheat to 300°F. Once the oven gets to temperature, remove the baking sheet, cover with foil or parchment and add the pizza. Cover the top loosely with foil, return to the oven, and let it go until the crust is crisp and the cheese is melty. Again, check it often so that it doesn't dry out or burn.

CHEF SARA'S TOP TIPS

I've heard excuses from clients and patients my whole career. "I can't work out because I don't have enough time"; "I can't buy tomatoes because I don't know how to pick them out at the grocery store"; "I can't cook, so I have to eat out at restaurants."

Listen, excuses are just a way to get out of doing things, usually things you don't like to do. Find time to work out because your health depends on it, learn how to pick the right tomato because you deserve a delicious tomato in your salad, and learn to cook so that you don't have to pay someone else to do it for you. Embrace the challenges and find ways to make the things you don't like to do enjoyable.

Too many people see pizza as something that takes too much time and requires too much effort or skill to make. Well, that's silly. You can absolutely make pizza, you just have to *want* to. And once you learn how, the pizza world will open its arms wide to you. So read all of the info in the previous pages (that I know you might have skipped over) and familiarize yourself with the process. Read and practice. Then practice, practice, practice. It's the only way you get better!

To help you get started, I'm adding a few special tips here just for you. Because you know I want you to succeed!

1. **Read the entire recipe before you start cooking.** This is imperative! Read it and then you'll be prepared and ready. That preparedness equals success!

2. **Experiment.** Say you look at one of my recipes and you're like, "Uh, um, no Sara." To that I say, "All good, friend!" That's right! If you don't dig it, don't make it. Or, better yet, swap some stuff and see what happens. Half the fun of cooking is experimenting!

3. **Don't give up.** This one goes with that whole paragraph above about excuses. It's super easy to give up and get angry and throw your dough ball in the trash. Instead, realize that failure is part of the process. Accept it. Take a deep breath and find a way to fix it. Or you know, just start over again.

4. **Have fun.** Nothing is enjoyable if it's not a little bit fun. Pizza-making should be fun. So, turn on the music, get dancing and make pizza.

5. **Embrace your limitations.** Don't have a smoking-hot pizza oven? Me neither! This book was written for the home cook, like you! Every problem has a work-around, you just have to find it. Same with the recipes in this book. If you don't have something, don't panic, find a replacement. Or don't and see what happens. It's just pizza.

READING THE RECIPES

THE *PIZZA! PIZZA! PIZZA!* METHOD

You'll find all my greatest pizza recipes here, but before you jump in, let's go over the ins and outs of the pizza prep process. Take a few minutes to read this over (I promise to be brief!) and use it for all of the pizza recipes in this book.

1. **Set up everything you're going to need ahead of time.** That means having your sauce and toppings ready to go because you'll need to work quickly. Dough that sits too long on your peel will stick. That's no fun.

2. **Start with pizza dough at room temperature.** Room temperature dough is easier to stretch and shape than cold dough. If yours is in the refrigerator, pull it out at least 45 minutes before you want to make your pizza. I usually go for an hour and set the dough in the covered bowl *near* my oven, but not on it or in it.

3. **Place your stone or steel in the cold oven before turning it on.** Your stone needs to be heated gradually, if you'll recall from our discussion about thermal shock (page 14). If you don't have a stone or steel, use an inverted baking sheet. Place it on the lowest rack in your oven. You'll be using that to put your pizza on in place of the stone or steel.

4. **Preheat the oven.** Preheat your oven to 500°F at least one hour before baking. Of course, you could do it for less time and it will likely work, but I've always done one hour and I've always been happy with the results!

5. **Prepare some extra flour (any kind) before you start playing with your dough.** I always keep my canister of all-purpose flour open and ready in case I need to grab some during the stretching of the dough.

6. **If you're making your dough on a pizza peel, throw a little flour on it along with some semolina or fine cornmeal and use your hand to coat it evenly.** I like a 50/50 combo of each. Make sure you have a good coating. This will help prevent your dough from sticking. If you're making your pizza on parchment paper, still do this, just on the parchment.

7. **Use your hands (or if absolutely necessary, a rolling pin).** I love using my hands to shape my dough. Doing so keeps all of those bubbles intact. A rolling pin will push them all out, deflating your dough. The only time I use a pin is for making a thin-crust pie.

8. **Turn your ball of dough out onto a clean work surface that has been dusted with flour.** Be sure to dust your hands in flour, too!

9. **Pick up the ball and start to lightly pull it apart, stretching it slightly in opposite directions.** Rotate it in both hands, holding onto it about 1 inch from the edges (the edges become your outer, puffy crust, so if you grab them too tightly here, you'll deflate them) and gently pull while letting the dough hang to allow it to stretch. I like this method because it allows gravity to do its thing. If you need a bit more stretch in the middle, you can move your hands underneath the dough. The dough should be big enough to cover the backs of both of your hands when placed in fists touching each other.

10. **Starting with your fists together (knuckles up), use your knuckles (*not* your fingers, as they'll poke holes in your dough) to pull the dough from the middle outward, rotating the dough around until you get a circle the size you want.** If you can't get a circle, don't worry about it. Your pizza will be delicious no matter what shape it is.

11. **Place the dough on your prepared peel or parchment.** Use floured fingers to push the dough out a bit more if it needs some extra reshaping. Stay away from the edges, that's your beautiful outer crust; you don't want to smash it! Just an FYI: the more you fuss with the dough, the tighter it will get, making it *super* hard to work with. So fuss a little, not a lot, okay?

12. **Add your toppings, but don't go crazy.** You need to move that pizza from the peel to a *very* hot oven, remember? Do a light coating of sauce and then have a light hand with the toppings. Shake the peel while you're topping your dough to make sure your pizza isn't sticking. And work fast, so your dough doesn't start to stick to it.

13. **Transfer your pizza to the stone or steel in your oven.** If you're using parchment, simply slide the pie and the parchment onto either the stone, steel or baking sheet and bake. If you're transferring from the peel to the stone, baking sheet or steel, then give it a few gentle shakes before you even think of opening the oven door. Working quickly, open the oven, pull the oven rack out a little so that you can easily access your stone/steel/baking sheet. Place the tip of your peel on the back (the side closest to the back of the oven) of the stone/steel/baking sheet and shimmy it off using a firm, but brief back and forth motion until it's completely transferred. (I recommend trying this a few times, once using a smaller size dough and one without any toppings. This is called practice and will help build your confidence.)

14. **Remove your pizza from the oven with the pizza peel, then transfer it to a cutting board before slicing.** *Never* slice your pizza on the peel; you'll destroy it.

15. **Slice, serve and enjoy!**

PREPPING FOR PERFECT PIZZA

I know you're probably excited, but here are just a few more notes before you get started:

- **The dough recipes** in this book are written to make *two* 10-inch pizzas.

- **The pizza recipes** are written to make *one* 10-inch pizza, except for the pan pizza, which requires you to use both dough balls.

- **Many of the sauces** for these pizzas can also be store-bought. If you don't have time to make them, just buy them.

- **Use your freezer!** There are plenty of sauces in this book that freeze well. Simply transfer to an ice cube tray or other silicone, freezer-safe food storage vessel and freeze. Pop out the cubes/blocks and place in a freezer-safe bag. Label and store in the freezer. You'll be able to pop out what you need when you need it!

- **Buy yourself a scale.** Not only will this help by taking the guesswork out of making your dough, but using it is way easier than scooping all of those ingredients. You can literally just set your mixing bowl on the scale and add your ingredients. No measuring cups to clean!

- **If you insist on not buying a scale, then please pay attention to how you measure your ingredients.** If you're measuring flour, I highly recommend using a spoon to transfer the flour to your measuring cup. Scooping will pack flour and you'll end up with more than you need. Use the spoon method and save yourself the annoyance. The same rules apply to liquid ingredients. Use a liquid measuring cup for water and oil and set it on a level surface to ensure you're filling it correctly.

- **There are lots of factors that can affect your dough.** You may follow my recipe exactly and still find your dough is too dry or too wet. Don't throw it at the wall in frustration; that's messy and uncalled for. Instead, fix it! If it's too wet, add a little more flour. If it's too dry, add a little more water. And remember, practice makes perfect!

- **Choose your own adventure.** I include two types of instructions for making your pizza dough. One is a mostly hands-off method where your stand mixer does all of the work, and the other is a hands-on method, no-knead method, which allows you to get your hands dirty. Both work well.

PIZZA PROBLEM-SOLVING & FAQS

Problem #1: The dough tears when I'm shaping it.

Ugh, so annoying! But all is not lost! Just pinch it together and finish shaping on your work surface. A little tear never hurt anyone.

Problem #2: My dough isn't a perfect circle.

That's cool! I prefer it when my dough isn't a circle; it looks way better and tastes way better, too. All kidding aside, the shape of your pizza doesn't matter as long as it fits on your pizza stone or steel.

Problem #3: The cheese won't melt.

Move your pizza to the top rack in your oven and switch it to broil. Broil until you get that dreamy, melted cheese you're after. Keep an eye on it, though; this shouldn't take too long, only a couple of minutes.

Problem #4: My dough won't stretch.

It's likely that you played with it a bit too much or it's too cold. No problem. Just cover it and let it rest for about 10–15 minutes and then come back to it.

The more you pull and shape it, the tighter the dough will get. That's why I like the pulling technique to shape my dough. And cold dough isn't pliable. Let the dough sit on the counter and allow it to get to room temperature before shaping.

Problem #5: Many recipes are vegetarian, but can they be vegan, too?

Yes! Many vegetarian recipes in the book can be made vegan, usually by swapping honey for sugar or agave nectar in the dough and by substituting your favorite vegan cheese equivalent for traditional mozzarella cheese and other cheeses mentioned in the recipe.

WINE AND . . . PIZZA?

Included in my culinary school curriculum was an "Introduction to Wine" course. I was 29 at the time and excited to learn more about wine and how it pairs with food. After that culinary school experience, wine was never the same for me. I now knew how to taste wine, how to "open" it, swirl it, sniff it, and aerate it when I took a sip to really experience it. By identifying what I was "tasting" in the wine, I was able to appreciate it that much more.

So what does all of this have to do with pizza? Well, for some of you, nothing. Perhaps you don't care at all about wine and that's totally fine. Maybe you dig a big glass of ice water with your pizza or an excellent craft beer. All good! I love those too. But for me, I love to pair my pizza with wine.

For that reason, I have enlisted the help of a few of my favorite wineries to pair some of the pizzas in this book. And while I love these pairings, the bottom line is always drink what you like! If you like Chardonnay with your spicy pepperoni pizza, do it! There really aren't any rules! Cheers and drink responsibly please! And don't miss my interview with Thomas Vogele of LUKE Wines on (page 179).

THE RECIPES

Dough & Crusts

34   Same Day Pizza Dough

36   Half & Half Same Day Dough

38   Next Day Pizza Dough

40   Gluten-Free Pizza Dough

Same Day Pizza Dough

MAKES: ENOUGH FOR TWO 10-INCH PIZZAS

Need a dough for when you want pizza today? This is it! Notice that this dough only uses all-purpose or bread flour, so if you're not a fan of whole grains in your dough or are just in the mood for something more basic, this is it.

1 rounded teaspoon (4 grams) active dry yeast

1 teaspoon (7 grams) honey

1 cup (237 grams) warm water (about 105°F–110°F), divided

3 cups (360 grams) unbleached all-purpose or bread flour

1 rounded teaspoon (7 grams) kosher salt

Mostly Hands-Off Method

Place yeast in a large mixing bowl or the bowl of a stand mixer. Add the honey and ¼ cup (60 grams) of the water and stir a few times to combine. Let sit until bubbling and foamy, about 5 minutes. Add the flour, salt and remaining water, and stir with a wooden spoon or the dough hook of a stand mixer until just combined. Cover with a towel and let rest for 20 minutes. Uncover, and if using a stand mixer, use the dough hook and knead on low speed until smooth and firm, about 5 minutes. If kneading by hand, transfer dough ball to a lightly floured kitchen countertop and knead 8 minutes.

If you're making the pizza in the next hour or so, shape dough into two, equal-size balls and place on a floured surface. Cover loosely with a clean tea towel or piece of plastic wrap and let rest in a draft-free spot until doubled in size, 1–1½ hours.

If not making pizza in the next hour or so, shape dough into a ball and place in a large, food-safe container or bowl (preferably one with a lid) coated with non-stick cooking spray or olive oil. Cover with the lid or plastic wrap and refrigerate until ready to make. (I like to do this early in the day if I can because the refrigerator fermentation makes for a more flavorful crust. But any amount of refrigeration is great!)

Hands-On, No-Knead Method

Place yeast in a large mixing bowl and add the honey and ¼ cup (60 grams) of the water. Let sit until bubbling and foamy, about 5 minutes. Add the flour, salt, and remaining water, and stir with a wooden spoon or until combined. Then, using your hands, start to work it into a ball and pick up any loose flour as you go. Once fully combined, shape into a ball. Return to the bowl, cover with a tea towel or plastic wrap and let sit on the counter for 20 minutes. Uncover, transfer dough ball to the counter, pick it up, and grabbing it from opposite ends, gently pull apart, then fold ends to meet in the center. Turn it 90 degrees and repeat the process. The dough won't want to be pulled too far, so don't get overly-aggressive.

Flip the dough over and place on a clean work surface. Rotating as you go, pull the edges and "tuck" the dough under itself to create a smooth, round ball. Place the ball back into the bowl, cover and rest 20 minutes. Repeat the process two more times, but after the last stretch, divide and shape into two balls, return to bowl, cover, and refrigerate until at least 45 minutes before baking.

TECHNIQUE NOTE: The more you make dough, the easier it will get! While this recipe should yield good results without much hassle, there may be times when the dough is too wet/sticky or even too dry. In those cases, add a little more flour (a tablespoon at a time) or water (a tablespoon at a time), until the dough is workable.

INGREDIENT NOTE: For all of the wheat-based doughs in this book, all-purpose flour will produce a crispier crust, but can also tear more easily (thanks to its lower gluten content). Bread flour will produce a chewier crust and is easier than all-purpose flour to shape and stretch. You can use either in this recipe or a combination of the two. Keep dough covered while it proofs. Leaving it uncovered will cause it to dry out.

MAKE IT VEGAN: For both methods, substitute an equal amount of sugar or agave nectar for honey.

Half & Half Same Day Dough

MAKES: TWO BALLS OF DOUGH, ENOUGH FOR TWO 10-INCH PIZZAS

This is the dough you want to use if you want your pizza today and you'd like it to include some whole grains. I've added a bit of honey and oil to this dough for both flavor and for making the dough user-friendly.

1 rounded teaspoon (4 grams) active dry yeast

1 tablespoon (21 grams) honey, divided

1 cup (237 grams) warm water (about 105°F–110°F), divided

1½ cups (180 grams) all-purpose flour

1½ cups (180 grams) whole wheat flour

1 rounded teaspoon (7 grams) kosher salt

1 tablespoon (15 grams) extra-virgin olive oil

Mostly Hands-Off Method

Place yeast in a large mixing bowl or the bowl of a stand mixer. Add 1 teaspoon (7 grams) honey and ¼ cup (60 grams) of the water and stir a few times to combine. Let sit until bubbling and foamy, about 5 minutes. Add the flour, salt, oil and remaining honey and water and stir with a wooden spoon or the dough hook of a stand mixer until just combined. Cover with a towel and let rest for 20 minutes. Uncover, and if using a stand mixer, use the dough hook and knead on low speed until smooth and firm, about 5 minutes. If mixing by hand, transfer dough ball to a lightly floured kitchen countertop and knead for 8 minutes.

If not making pizza in the next hour or so, shape dough into a ball and place in a large, food-safe container or bowl (preferably one with a lid) coated with non-stick cooking spray or olive oil. Cover with the lid or plastic wrap and refrigerate until ready to make. (I like to do this early in the day if I can because the refrigerator fermentation makes for a more flavorful crust. But any amount of refrigeration is great!)

If you're making the pizza in the next hour or so, divide and shape dough into two equal-size balls and place on a floured surface. Cover loosely with a clean tea towel or piece of plastic wrap and let rest in a draft-free space until doubled in size, 1–1½ hours.

Remove dough from the refrigerator at least 45 minutes before baking. Keep covered until ready to use.

Hands-On, No-Knead Method

Place yeast in a large mixing bowl and add the honey and ¼ cup (60 grams) of the water. Let sit until bubbling and foamy, about 5 minutes. Add the flour, salt and remaining water and stir with a wooden spoon or until combined.

Then, using your hands, start to work it into a ball and pick up any loose flour as you go. Once fully combined, shape into a ball. Return to the bowl, cover with a tea towel or plastic wrap, and let sit on the counter for 20 minutes. Uncover, transfer dough ball to counter, pick it up and, grabbing it from opposite ends, gently pull apart, then fold ends to meet in the center. Turn it 90 degrees and repeat the process. The dough won't want to be pulled too far, so don't get over-aggressive. Flip the dough over and place on a clean work surface. Using one or two cupped hands, pull it toward you to "tuck" the dough under itself. Rotate and repeat this process a few times to create a smooth top.

Place the ball back into the bowl, cover and rest 20 minutes. Repeat the process two more times, but after the last stretch, divide and shape into two balls, return to bowl, cover, and refrigerate until at least 45 minutes before baking.

MAKE IT VEGAN: For both methods, substitute an equal amount of sugar or agave nectar for honey.

Next Day Pizza Dough

MAKES: ENOUGH FOR TWO 10-INCH PIZZAS

If you're a planner, then I highly recommend using this dough. I like it because it gets a full day's worth of fermentation in the refrigerator. That means it's going to taste awesome and have perfect, beautiful air bubbles.

¼ rounded teaspoon (1 gram) active dry yeast

1 teaspoon (7 grams) plus 1 tablespoon (21 grams) honey, divided

1 cup (237 grams) warm water (about 105°F–110°F), divided

3 cups (360 grams) all-purpose flour (or combination of all-purpose flour and bread flour)

1 rounded teaspoon (7 grams) kosher salt

2 teaspoons (10 grams) extra-virgin olive oil

Mostly Hands-Off Method

Place yeast in a mixing bowl or the bowl of a stand mixer. Add the honey and ¼ cup of the water and stir a few times to combine. Let sit, until bubbling and foamy, about 5 minutes. Add the flour, salt, oil, and remaining water and stir with a wooden spoon or the dough hook of a stand mixer until just combined.

Cover with a towel and let rest for 20 minutes. Uncover, and if using a stand mixer, use the dough hook and knead on low speed until smooth and firm, about 5 minutes. If making by hand, transfer dough ball to a lightly floured kitchen countertop and knead for 8 minutes.

Coat a food-safe container or bowl (preferably one with a lid) with non-stick cooking spray or olive oil. Shape dough into two, equal-size balls (for two 10-inch pizzas) and place in the container. Cover with the lid or plastic wrap and refrigerate overnight (up to 72 hours).

Remove dough from the refrigerator at least 45 minutes before baking. Keep covered until ready to use.

Hands-On, No-Knead Method

Place yeast in a mixing bowl and add the honey and ¼ cup of the water. Let sit until bubbling and foamy, about 5 minutes. Add the flour, salt and remaining water and stir with a wooden spoon or until combined. Pick up the dough and shape into a ball. Return to the bowl, cover with a tea towel or plastic wrap and let sit on the counter for 20 minutes.

Uncover, transfer dough ball to counter, pick it up and, grabbing it from opposite ends, gently pull apart, then fold ends to meet in the center. Turn it 90 degrees and repeat the process. Flip the dough over and shape into a ball. Place back into the bowl, cover and rest for 20 minutes. Repeat the process two more times, but after the last stretch, shape into two balls (for two 10-inch pizzas), place in a large, food-safe container or bowl (preferably one with a lid) coated with non-stick cooking spray or olive oil, cover, and refrigerate at least 24 hours and up to 72 hours.

INGREDIENT NOTE: Make this dough whole grain by swapping half of the all-purpose flour for whole wheat flour.

MAKE IT VEGAN: For both methods, substitute an equal amount of sugar or agave nectar for honey.

Gluten-Free Pizza Dough

MAKES: TWO BALLS OF DOUGH, ENOUGH FOR TWO 10-INCH PIZZAS

While I don't have celiac disease or a gluten-sensitivity, I know that many people do, and I know that they love pizza just as much as me. That's why I reached out to my friend, Jenny Passione, MS, RD, CC, a colleague and owner of Olive Lane Culinary Nutrition, who has celiac disease and specializes in gluten-free and allergy-friendly recipes, to help me create a yummy GF pizza dough.

2¼ teaspoons (7 grams) instant or active dry yeast

1 cup (237 grams) warm water (about 105°F–110°F), divided

1 teaspoon (7 grams) plus 1 tablespoon (21 grams) honey, divided

2 cups (296 grams) gluten-free flour blend

2 teaspoons xanthan gum

1 teaspoon apple cider vinegar

1 teaspoon kosher salt

¼ cup extra-virgin olive oil, divided

Stir yeast, ¼ cup water and 1 teaspoon honey together in a bowl and let sit until bubbly, 5 minutes. Add remaining water and honey along with flour, xanthan gum, vinegar, salt and 2 tablespoons oil. Stir until combined, then using wet hands, a wooden spoon or a spatula, shape into two balls. The mixture will be sticky. Transfer dough balls to a baking sheet that has been lightly coated with gluten-free flour. Dust tops with a little more gluten-free flour. Cover dough balls with plastic wrap or a clean tea towel and let them rise until a bit puffy, about 1–1½ hours. (NOTE: this GF pizza dough won't rise like dough made with wheat flour, so don't expect it to double in size. Instead, it should grow a bit in size and appear lighter and puffier than before the rise.)

Place a piece of parchment on a pizza peel, cutting board or inverted baking sheet. Drizzle 1 tablespoon oil on the parchment. Use your fingers to evenly coat the parchment with oil in the area where you'll be making your pizza. Remove 1 ball of dough and press it into shape using lightly oiled or wet hands (keep a bowl of water handy so that you can keep your hands wet). Use your wet hands to repair any cracks and to seal any parts that appear rough. Repeat the process with the remaining ball of dough. Partially bake at 500°F until lightly golden, about 10–12 minutes.

Remove from oven, add sauce and desired toppings, and bake until cheese is melted and bubbling, about 8–10 minutes.

INGREDIENT NOTE: When looking for a gluten-free flour blend for pizza, I recommend choosing one that has xanthan gum in it. Xanthan gum mimics what gluten does by helping with binding ingredients and developing structure. I add a little extra here for insurance purposes, but if you can't find it, don't worry about it.

MAKE IT VEGAN: For both methods, substitute an equal amount of sugar or agave nectar for honey.

Sauces

45   Homemade Pizza Sauce

46   Crushed Tomato & Basil Sauce

49   Roasted Red Pepper Sauce

50   Olive & Sun-Dried Tomato Tapenade

53   Pistachio Chimichurri

54   Basil Pesto

56   Spicy Cilantro Oil

57   Easy BBQ Sauce

58   Hummus

61   Fire-Roasted Tomato Salsa

62   Sara's Buttermilk Ranch

Homemade Pizza Sauce

MAKES: A GENEROUS CUP

You can buy pizza sauce and many of your options are great. But I believe that once you make your own, you'll never go back to the store-bought stuff!

---

1 (15-ounce) can diced tomatoes

2 teaspoons extra-virgin olive oil

¼ cup chopped yellow onion

2 cloves garlic, minced

2 tablespoons tomato paste

2 tablespoons balsamic vinegar, divided

2 teaspoons Italian seasoning

¼ teaspoon kosher salt

¼ teaspoon black pepper

Drain tomatoes, reserving the juice. Set aside.

Heat the oil in a large saucepan over medium-low heat. Add the onions and cook until softened and golden, stirring often, about 4–5 minutes. Add garlic and cook until fragrant, about 30 seconds. Add the tomato paste, and cook, stirring often, until brick red, about 4 minutes. Stir in 1 tablespoon vinegar and the reserved tomato juice, turn heat to medium and cook until slightly thickened, about 2 minutes. Add the drained tomatoes and Italian seasoning and bring to a boil. Reduce heat to low and simmer, uncovered, until sauce has thickened, about 20 minutes.

Stir in salt, black pepper, and the remaining tablespoon of vinegar.

Let cool slightly, then blend with an immersion blender or by carefully transferring to a blender and pureeing until smooth.

COOKING NOTE: Simmer longer, up to 1 hour, for deeper flavor.

INGREDIENT NOTE: If you have fresh basil on hand, add ¼ cup just before blending.

STORAGE INFO: Refrigerate for up to five days or freeze for up to 6 months.

NOTE: Spicy Pizza Sauce: Prepare as above but add 1–2 teaspoons crushed red pepper when adding diced tomatoes and Italian seasoning. Proceed with recipe.

NOTE: Veggie-Packed Pizza Sauce: Add ¼ cup diced carrots, ¼ cup diced celery, ¼ cup zucchini, and ¼ cup yellow squash along with onions, or use 1 cup chopped veggies of your choice. Cook until softened, about 10 minutes. Proceed with recipe.

Crushed Tomato & Basil Sauce

MAKES: ABOUT 1½ CUPS

This sauce is my all-time favorite of all of the sauces. Why? Because it's simple to make, yet tastes so delicious! It's the perfect base for many of the recipes in this book.

1 (28-ounce) can whole, peeled tomatoes, preferably San Marzano, drained

1 tablespoon extra-virgin olive oil

2 cloves garlic

½ teaspoon dried oregano leaves

1 cup fresh basil, torn

¼ teaspoon kosher salt

⅛ teaspoon black pepper

Break tomatoes apart with your hands, remove and discard seeds, and add to a blender or the bowl of a food processor. Add remaining ingredients and blend until smooth.

INGREDIENT NOTE: Any canned, whole tomatoes will work, so feel free to use whatever you can find at your store. I prefer San Marzano because they have a deep, super-luscious tomato flavor.

BRIGHT IDEA: Save tomato liquid for another use. I like to use it for soups, salad dressings and marinades.

STORAGE INFO: Refrigerate for up to five days or freeze for up to 6 months.

Roasted Red Pepper Sauce

MAKES: ABOUT 1¼ CUPS

If you're anything like me, you need an occasional break from the all-tomato pizza sauce. Enter this roasted red pepper sauce. It's a simple recipe, but packs so much flavor! I use it for several recipes in the book, but honestly, it's really great on just about anything.

---

2 jarred roasted red bell peppers (about 8 ounces), roughly chopped

2 cloves garlic

1 tablespoon red wine vinegar

¼ teaspoon crushed red pepper

1 tablespoon fresh oregano leaves or ¼ teaspoon dried

¼ cup extra-virgin olive oil

¼ teaspoon kosher salt

⅛ teaspoon black pepper

Add all ingredients to a blender or bowl of a food processor and blend until smooth.

RECIPE NOTE: Add a fresh herb, such as 1 cup of fresh basil before blending.

STORAGE INFO: Refrigerate for up to five days or freeze for up to 6 months.

Olive & Sun-Dried Tomato Tapenade

MAKES: A GENEROUS CUP

I love a good hit of salt, especially the briny-kind you get from olives! This tapenade makes for a fun and unique sauce for pizza. It's so good, you might want to scoop it up on a cracker and enjoy it that way too!

---

1 cup pitted kalamata olives, drained

½ cup slivered oil-packed, sun-dried tomatoes

2 tablespoons raisins

1 cup lightly packed fresh flat-leaf parsley, chopped

1 tablespoon fresh oregano leaves or ¼ teaspoon dried

1 tablespoon red wine vinegar

¼ cup extra-virgin olive oil

Add the olives, sun-dried tomatoes, raisins, parsley and oregano to a small food processor and pulse until roughly chopped. Remove lid, scrape down the sides of the bowl and add vinegar and olive oil; pulse to combine.

RECIPE NOTE: Substitute cranberries or dried cherries for raisins.

STORAGE INFO: Refrigerate for up to five days.

Pistachio Chimichurri

MAKES: ½ CUP

Chimichurri is a favorite sauce of mine. You know I love simplicity, and this one is simple. It's a sauce that hails from Argentina and is typically loaded with fresh herbs, vinegar, oil and spices. My version is vinegar-forward and has a hit of pistachios for a creamier texture, which makes for a great pizza sauce.

¼ cup lightly salted pistachios, roughly chopped

1 cup packed fresh flat-leaf parsley (leaves and stems), torn

1 tablespoon fresh oregano leaves or ¼ teaspoon dried

¼ teaspoon crushed red pepper

2 cloves garlic, roughly chopped

1–2 tablespoons red wine vinegar, to taste

⅛ teaspoon kosher salt

⅛ teaspoon black pepper

⅓ cup extra-virgin olive oil

Add the pistachios, parsley, oregano, crushed red pepper, garlic, 1 tablespoon vinegar, salt, and black pepper to a food processor and pulse until roughly chopped, 15–20 seconds. Remove lid and scrape down the sides of the bowl. With food processor running, stream in olive oil and blend to desired consistency. Taste, and add additional tablespoon vinegar if desired, blending to combine.

RECIPE NOTE: Other nuts or seeds can be used in place of pistachios, such as cashews, almonds, pumpkin seeds, or sunflower seeds.

STORAGE INFO: Refrigerate for up to five days.

Basil Pesto

MAKES: ⅔ CUP

It wouldn't be a pizza cookbook without a pesto sauce, right? My version is pretty traditional, but I encourage you to experiment with different nuts, and even swap in some other herbs or greens for the basil!

¼ cup pine nuts

¼ cup freshly grated Parmesan or pecorino cheese

2 cloves fresh garlic

3 cups lightly packed fresh basil leaves

½ cup extra-virgin olive oil

½ teaspoon lemon zest

¼ teaspoon kosher salt

⅛ teaspoon black pepper

Crushed red pepper to taste (optional)

Place pine nuts in a dry skillet set over medium-low heat. Cook, stirring often, until lightly browned and fragrant, about 3–5 minutes. Remove from skillet and let cool.

Add nuts, cheese and garlic to the bowl of a small food processor and pulse until roughly chopped, about 15 seconds. Add the basil, cover with the lid and, with food processor running, stream in the olive oil, stopping to scrape down the sides of the bowl as needed, until fully combined, about 1 minute. Stir in lemon zest, salt, black pepper and crushed red pepper, if using.

INGREDIENT NOTE: Pre-shredded cheese makes life easy here, but I prefer to grate my own. Manufacturers add ingredients to pre-shredded/grated cheeses to keep them from clumping and I don't want those in my pesto!

RECIPE NOTE: Pine nuts can sometimes be expensive or hard to find. Luckily, almost any nut is a good substitute. I love using cashews here for their mild flavor, but you could use almonds, walnuts and even pistachios.

RECIPE NOTE: Swap some of the green in your pesto by substituting 1 cup spinach or kale for the basil.

COOKING NOTE: Texture here is up to you! If you like your pesto a little more rustic, don't process very long. If you want your pesto smooth and creamy, go as long as you need to get there.

STORAGE INFO: Add a glug of oil to the top of the pesto before you refrigerate. This will create a barrier between the pesto and the air, which will help keep that pesto green! Refrigerate for up to five days or freeze for up to three months.

Spicy Cilantro Oil

MAKES: ABOUT ½ CUP

I use this sauce all of the time at home. It's perfect for pizza, but it also makes for a great marinade, salad dressing or topping for tacos!

---

1 cup packed fresh cilantro leaves and stems, roughly chopped

2 cloves garlic, roughly chopped

2 tablespoons roughly chopped jalapeño (about 1 pepper)

½ teaspoon ground coriander

¼ teaspoon kosher salt

⅓ cup avocado oil (or canola oil)

Add the cilantro, garlic and jalapeño to a food processor and pulse to combine. Remove lid, scrape down sides of the bowl and add the coriander and salt. Cover with the lid and, with the processor running, stream in oil and blend until smooth.

INGREDIENT NOTE: If you're looking for less spice, remove jalapeño seeds before chopping.

STORAGE INFO: Refrigerate for up to five days or freeze for up to three months.

Easy BBQ Sauce

MAKES: ABOUT ½ CUP

I know what you're thinking, is this really easy? My answer is, "Yes! Of course!" Usually, homemade BBQ sauce takes hours to prepare. Not this one! All you need is 30 minutes and you've got a delicious sauce that rivals anything you can find at the store!

½ cup ketchup

¼ cup water

2 tablespoons yellow mustard

⅓ cup apple juice or apple cider

1 tablespoon molasses

1 tablespoon Worcestershire sauce

2 tablespoons packed brown sugar

1 tablespoon honey

1 teaspoon smoked paprika

1 teaspoon garlic powder

1 teaspoon onion powder

⅛ teaspoon crushed red pepper

1 tablespoon apple cider vinegar

Combine all ingredients except for the apple cider vinegar in a small pot and bring to a simmer over medium heat. Reduce heat to low and simmer, stirring often, until thickened, about 25–30 minutes.

Remove from heat and stir in the apple cider vinegar.

INGREDIENT NOTE: For a less sweet sauce, use a lesser amount of brown sugar.

STORAGE NOTE: Refrigerate for up to five days.

Hummus

MAKES: ABOUT 3 CUPS

I highly recommend blending up a batch of homemade hummus. Not only can you use it as a topping for pizza (it's delicious), but you can also enjoy it as a snack with pita chips and your favorite veggies!

2 (15-ounce) cans garbanzo beans, drained and rinsed

2 tablespoons tahini

¼ cup fresh lemon juice (from 2 lemons)

2 cloves roasted garlic or 2 cloves garlic (see Note)

1 teaspoon ground cumin

⅛ teaspoon cayenne pepper

½ teaspoon kosher salt

⅛ teaspoon black pepper

¼ cup extra-virgin olive oil plus extra for garnish

Ice water to thin, as needed

Add the garbanzo beans, tahini, lemon juice, garlic, cumin, cayenne pepper, salt, and black pepper to the bowl of a food processor and pulse to combine. Scrape down the sides of the bowl. With the processor running, stream in olive oil and blend until smooth. Add water, 1 tablespoon at a time as needed to create a smooth consistency.

Remove mixture to a bowl and drizzle with olive oil as garnish, if desired.

INGREDIENT NOTE: If you're crunched for time, you can skip roasting the garlic. Raw garlic works here too. Roasted garlic provides a more mellow, almost sweet garlic flavor than raw, which is more punchy and bold. The choice is yours!

TO ROAST GARLIC: Preheat the oven to 425°F. Slice off the top of one head of garlic to expose the cloves and place it, cut end up, on a piece of foil, then drizzle with 1 teaspoon of olive oil. Fold up the sides of the foil and loosely close at the top. Place on a baking sheet or directly on the rack in the oven. Roast until tender, about 25–30 minutes. Let cool, then remove roasted garlic from their skins.

STORAGE INFO: Refrigerate for up to five days.

Fire-Roasted Tomato Salsa

MAKES: 1½ CUPS

You may or may not know this, but I wrote a cookbook all about tacos. I love them! And I love all of the ingredients that go inside of them. This recipe is in that book, but I'm adding it here too because—surprise! It makes for a delicious sauce for pizza!

½ medium white onion, quartered

1 jalapeño, sliced in half lengthwise, then quartered

2 cloves garlic

1 tablespoon extra-virgin olive oil

1 (14.5-ounce) can fire-roasted diced tomatoes, drained

½ cup packed fresh cilantro (see Note)

2 tablespoons fresh lime juice (about one lime)

¼ teaspoon kosher salt

Preheat the oven to broil and line a rimmed baking sheet with foil. Add the onion, jalapeño and garlic to the pan, drizzle with oil and toss with clean hands.

Broil, stirring occasionally, until vegetables are tender and start to blister, about 5 minutes.

Allow vegetables to cool slightly, then transfer to a food processor or blender. Add the drained tomatoes, cilantro, lime juice and salt. Puree until smooth.

INGREDIENT NOTE: The stems of cilantro are just as yummy as the leaves, so use them both for this recipe.

STORAGE INFO: Refrigerate for up to five days.

Sara's Buttermilk Ranch

MAKES: 1½ CUPS

Growing up in the Midwest meant ranch dressing had *to be served at every meal. If there was even a mention of salad, ranch would be there. Eventually, it just became a "thing"; you might need it on your spaghetti or to top your taco. For us, it's a versatile condiment we can't live without. You can buy it, but homemade tastes way better. Here's my version.*

⅔ cup low-fat buttermilk

1 cup olive oil mayonnaise

¼ cup chopped fresh chives

2 tablespoons chopped fresh dill

3 cloves garlic, roughly chopped

2 tablespoons fresh lemon juice (from 1 lemon)

¼ teaspoon kosher salt

⅛ teaspoon black pepper

Place all ingredients in a blender or small food processor and puree until smooth.

RECIPE NOTE: Spice it up by adding a few splashes of sriracha or other hot sauce. Or add a canned chipotle chile or half an avocado before blending.

STORAGE INFO: Refrigerate for up to five days.

Vegetarian Pizza

67   Spicy Southwest

68   Lemon, Shaved Parmesan & Arugula

71   Pepperoncini Peppers, Shredded Kale & Roasted Red Peppers

72   Grilled Vegetable Pizza

74   Sauteed Garlic Greens

75   Harissa, Chickpeas & Cilantro

76   Sun-Dried Tomato, Feta, Kalamata & Spinach

79   Simple Margarita

80   Roasted Tomato Margarita

83   Spinach, Hearts of Palm & Feta

84   Roasted Mushroom & Goat Cheese

86   Asparagus & Pistachio

89   Ricotta, Balsamic Onions & Pecans

90   Giardiniera & Spinach

93   Olive Tapenade

94   Asparagus, Artichoke Hearts & Capers

96   Hominy, Poblano & Cilantro

99   BBQ Kale

100   Peach & Jalapeño

103   Capers, Sun-Dried Tomatoes & Basil

104   Pistachio Chimichurri & Ricotta

107   Brussels Sprouts & Pecorino

108   Pesto, Spinach & Basil Goat Cheese

111   Hummus & Roasted Red Pepper

112   Green Olive & Chimichurri

115   Double-Dough Pan Pizza

116   Thin Crust

Spicy Southwest

MAKES: ONE 10-INCH PIZZA

The flavors that come from the southwest region of the United States are some of my most favorite. This recipe is first for a reason—it could be my favorite, but I'll never tell. Regardless, I hope you love it as much as I do.

Take this recipe up a notch by buying fresh corn on the cob and grilling or roasting it before adding to this pizza for a little smoky flavor. If fresh corn isn't at your grocery store, substitute with thawed, frozen sweet corn.

---

1 ball dough of your choice, at room temperature

3 tablespoons Spicy Cilantro Oil (page 56), divided

1 small jalapeño, sliced

⅓ cup canned black beans, drained and rinsed

¼ cup fresh sweet corn kernels

¼ cup seeded finely chopped fresh tomatoes

2 green onions, thinly sliced, divided

¼ teaspoon kosher salt

⅛ teaspoon black pepper

1 cup shredded pepper Jack cheese (4 ounces)

¼ cup fresh cilantro, chopped

Place pizza stone on lowest rack in the oven or, if using a steel, place on the highest rack. Preheat oven to 500°F at least 45 minutes to 1 hour before baking.

Sprinkle a bit of fine cornmeal and all-purpose flour on a pizza peel or piece of parchment. Stretch out the dough and shape into a circle (see page 22), then transfer to prepared peel or parchment. Spread 2 tablespoons of the cilantro oil over dough, leaving a 1-inch border around the edge, then top with jalapeño slices, black beans, corn, tomatoes, and half of the green onions. Sprinkle with salt and black pepper and scatter cheese on top.

Bake until the cheese is melted and the crust is golden, 8–10 minutes.

Remove the pizza from the oven and transfer it to a cutting board. Drizzle the remaining tablespoon of Spicy Cilantro Oil on top, and garnish with the cilantro and remaining green onions. Cut into slices and enjoy immediately.

INGREDIENT TIP: Fresh tomatoes can be a bit watery. Water doesn't make for a great pizza topping. If you have time, place the diced tomatoes in a strainer to allow some of the water to drain off or pat with a clean paper towel.

Lemon, Shaved Parmesan & Arugula

MAKES: ONE 10-INCH PIZZA

Shortly after I moved to Chicago, I went to a restaurant and ordered a pizza where they put a bunch of arugula on top after baking it. It blew my mind! I'm sharing my version here with you and honestly, it still *blows my mind!*

---

2 tablespoons extra-virgin olive oil

2 cloves garlic, thinly sliced

1 ball dough of your choice, at room temperature

4 ounces fresh mozzarella, sliced

⅛ teaspoon kosher salt

¼ teaspoon black pepper, divided

1 (5-ounce) package baby arugula (about 3 cups)

1 teaspoon lemon zest plus 1 tablespoon lemon juice (from 1 lemon)

1 tablespoon toasted pine nuts, optional

½ cup shaved Parmesan cheese

Place pizza stone on lowest rack in the oven or, if using a steel, place on the highest rack. Preheat oven to 500°F at least 45 minutes to 1 hour before baking.

Heat the oil in a small skillet over low heat. Add garlic and cook, stirring frequently, until fragrant, 5 minutes. Remove from heat and set aside.

Sprinkle a bit of fine cornmeal and all-purpose flour on a pizza peel or piece of parchment. Stretch out the dough and shape into a circle (see page 22). Transfer to prepared peel or parchment. Spread 2 tablespoons of garlic oil over the dough, then top with sliced mozzarella. Sprinkle with salt and ⅛ teaspoon black pepper.

Bake until the cheese is melted and the crust is golden, 8–10 minutes.

Toss the arugula, lemon zest, lemon juice, remaining ⅛ teaspoon black pepper and reserved garlic oil together in a large bowl. Set aside.

Remove the pizza from the oven and transfer it to a cutting board. Cut into slices, then top with arugula mixture, pine nuts, if using, and shaved Parmesan. Enjoy immediately.

COOKING TIP: To toast pine nuts, place them in a dry skillet set over medium-low heat. Cook, stirring often until lightly browned and fragrant, about 3–5 minutes. Remove from skillet and let cool.

TECHNIQUE TIP: Buy a block of Parmesan cheese instead of pre-shredded or grated, and use a vegetable peeler to create big, beautiful shavings to garnish this pizza.

WINE PAIRING: Cannonball's Chardonnay and Bread & Butter DOC Prosecco

Pepperoncini Peppers, Shredded Kale & Roasted Red Peppers

MAKES: ONE 10-INCH PIZZA

I firmly believe that jarred pepperoncini peppers are an overlooked food. They add heat, tang and punchiness to any dish! I love them paired with kale and roasted red peppers; they balance the earthiness from the kale and the creaminess from the roasted red peppers.

If you can't find lacinato (dinosaur) kale, curly kale is a fine substitute. Just be sure to give it a good scrub (see below) before using it.

1 ball dough of your choice, at room temperature

2 tablespoons **Spicy Pizza Sauce (page 45)**

1½ cups thinly sliced kale, preferably lacinato or dinosaur (see Prep Tip)

¼ cup mild or hot jarred sliced pepperoncini peppers

½ cup chopped jarred roasted red bell pepper, rinsed

1 cup low-moisture part-skim shredded mozzarella cheese (4 ounces)

¼ cup crumbled goat cheese

¼ teaspoon kosher salt

⅛ teaspoon black pepper

Place pizza stone on lowest rack in the oven or, if using a steel, place on the highest rack. Preheat oven to 500°F at least 45 minutes to 1 hour before baking.

Sprinkle a bit of fine cornmeal and all-purpose flour on a pizza peel or piece of parchment. Stretch out the dough and shape into a circle (see page 22), then transfer to prepared peel or parchment. Spread pizza sauce over dough leaving a 1-inch border around the edge, then top with kale, pepperoncini peppers and red peppers. Sprinkle mozzarella and goat cheese over the top and sprinkle with salt and black pepper.

Bake until the cheese is melted and the crust is golden, 8–10 minutes.

Remove the pizza from the oven and transfer it to a cutting board. Cut into slices and enjoy immediately.

PREP TIP: To clean and prep kale, strip kale leaves from the stem, tear into pieces, then add to a large bowl of cold water. Massage the leaves to help remove any dirt or debris. Gently lift out of the water and into a salad spinner or place on a clean towel. Spin or pat dry.

Grilled Vegetable Pizza

MAKES: TWO 10-INCH PIZZAS

On a summer day, there's nothing I love more than grilling! I'm a huge fan of grilling up a ton of veggies to throw on anything and put in everything! While I do have certain veggies listed here, feel free to grill up your own favorites for a truly customized version of this pizza.

Like most recipes in this book, this one is incredibly versatile! Swap the sauce for Basil Pesto (see page 54) or Spicy Pizza Sauce (see page 45) or whatever you like. Same goes for the veggies. Try eggplant or broccoli or whatever is on sale at your store.

---

1 large portobello mushroom cap, gills and stems removed

1 red bell pepper, cored and quartered lengthwise

1 green bell pepper, cored and quartered lengthwise

1 small zucchini, halved lengthwise

1 small yellow squash, halved lengthwise

½ small red onion, cut into ½-inch rounds (see Note)

¼ cup extra-virgin olive oil

¼ teaspoon kosher salt

¼ teaspoon black pepper

2 balls dough of your choice, at room temperature

¼ cup **Crushed Tomato & Basil Sauce (page 56)**

8 ounces fresh mozzarella

1 cup fresh basil leaves, torn

Place pizza stone on lowest rack in the oven or, if using a steel, place on the highest rack. Preheat oven to 500°F at least 45 minutes to 1 hour before baking.

Preheat the grill to medium-high. Clean and oil the grates.

Toss the mushroom, bell peppers, zucchini, squash and red onion with the oil, salt, and black pepper.

Place mushroom on prepared grill, gill side up and cook for 5 minutes. Flip the mushroom and add remaining veggies to the grill. Grill the mushroom and vegetables until tender and lightly charred, 5–7 minutes, flipping once halfway through cooking time. Remove from grill and let cool slightly. Transfer to a cutting board and chop into bite-size pieces.

Sprinkle a bit of fine cornmeal and all-purpose flour on a pizza peel or piece of parchment. Stretch out one ball of dough and shape into a circle (see page 22). Transfer to prepared peel or parchment. Spread 2 tablespoons sauce over the dough then top with half of the grilled veggies and cheese. Repeat the process with the other ball of dough and remaining sauce and ingredients.

Bake until the cheese is melted and the crust is golden, 8–10 minutes.

Remove pizzas from the oven and transfer to a cutting board. Garnish with basil, cut into slices and enjoy immediately.

COOKING NOTE: If you have more than one stone or steel, you can cook these pizzas at the same time. If not, just cook one at a time.

COOKING NOTE: Worried about your onion slices falling through the grill grates? Thread them onto metal or soaked wooden skewers before grilling!

COOKING NOTE: Want to cook the whole thing on the grill? Grab the method in the Pesto Grilled Chicken recipe on page 122.

Sautéed Garlic Greens

MAKES: ONE 10-INCH PIZZA

Garlic and greens are such a great pairing. While greens are typically served as a side dish, I find that they're truly lovely on pizza! I think you'll agree.

2 tablespoons extra-virgin olive oil

1 shallot, thinly sliced

3 cloves garlic, minced

8 cups thinly sliced greens (kale, mustard, collards, Swiss chard), about 1 bunch

1 (14.5-ounce) can diced tomatoes, drained (about 1 cup)

½ teaspoon crushed red pepper

¼ teaspoon kosher salt

⅛ teaspoon black pepper plus extra for garnishing

1 ball dough of your choice, at room temperature

1 cup low-moisture part-skim shredded mozzarella cheese (4 ounces)

½ cup shaved Parmesan cheese, plus extra for garnishing

Place pizza stone on lowest rack in the oven or, if using a steel, place on the highest rack. Preheat oven to 500°F at least 45 minutes to 1 hour before baking.

Heat oil in a large, heavy skillet, such as cast iron, set over medium heat. Add shallot, and cook, stirring often, until softened, 3 minutes. Add garlic and cook until fragrant, about 30 seconds. Add greens and cook until just starting to wilt, 1 minute. Stir in 2 tablespoons water, then reduce heat to a simmer. Cover with a lid or piece of foil and cook until greens are tender, about 5 minutes. Drain any excess liquid, then stir in the drained, diced tomatoes, crushed red pepper, salt and black pepper.

Sprinkle a bit of fine cornmeal and all-purpose flour on a pizza peel or piece of parchment. Stretch out the dough and shape into a circle (see page 22), then transfer to prepared peel or parchment. Cover with cooked greens, then sprinkle mozzarella and Parmesan cheese on top.

Bake until the cheese is melted and the crust is golden, 8–10 minutes.

Remove the pizza from the oven and transfer it to a cutting board. Garnish with black pepper and Parmesan cheese. Cut into slices and enjoy immediately.

RECIPE NOTE: Omit the mozzarella and just use Parmesan cheese or even crumbled feta cheese so that you can really enjoy those greens!

BREAKFAST-STYLE RECIPE NOTE: If you have eggs in your fridge, consider adding a few to this pizza! Make 3–4 indentations in the greens and add an egg to each. Bake normally, then slice and enjoy!

Harissa, Chickpeas & Cilantro

MAKES: ONE 10-INCH PIZZA

This pizza is outrageous! Just like me. It's a bunch of flavors and ingredients that I love though, so I figured, why not try them on a pizza. While I love harissa seasoning, I know it can be hard to find. If you can't get your hands on it, just skip it or substitute chili powder and proceed with the recipe as written.

1 cup canned chickpeas, rinsed

1 tablespoon extra-virgin olive oil

3 teaspoons dried harissa seasoning, divided

¼ teaspoon kosher salt

1 ball dough of your choice, at room temperature

2 tablespoons Roasted Red Pepper Sauce (page 49)

1 jarred roasted red bell pepper, chopped

1 cup low-moisture part-skim shredded mozzarella cheese (4 ounces)

¼ cup crumbled feta cheese

2 tablespoons plain Greek yogurt

1 teaspoon fresh lemon juice (from 1 lemon)

½ cup fresh cilantro, chopped

Crushed red pepper, Aleppo pepper or raisins, for garnishing (optional)

Place pizza stone on lowest rack in the oven or, if using a steel, place on the highest rack. Preheat oven to 500°F at least 45 minutes to 1 hour before baking.

Toss chickpeas with oil, 2 teaspoons harissa seasoning and salt. Set aside.

Sprinkle a bit of fine cornmeal and all-purpose flour on a pizza peel or piece of parchment. Stretch out the dough and shape into a circle (see page 22), then transfer to prepared peel or parchment. Spread red pepper sauce over dough leaving a 1-inch border around the edge, then top with roasted red bell peppers. Sprinkle mozzarella and feta cheese on top, then add chickpeas.

Bake until the cheese is melted and the crust is golden, 8–10 minutes.

Meanwhile, combine the remaining teaspoon harissa with the yogurt and the lemon juice in a small bowl.

Remove pizza from oven and transfer to a cutting board. Cut into slices, then drizzle with harissa-yogurt just before serving. Garnish with cilantro and crushed red pepper.

Sun-Dried Tomato, Feta, Kalamata & Spinach

MAKES: ONE 10-INCH PIZZA

Sometimes I picture myself vacationing in Greece, and during that daydream, I picture myself popping an endless number of kalamata olives in my mouth. That's because they are easily one of my most favorite foods! All of that yummy, salty, brininess makes me so happy! I love them on this pizza paired with sun-dried tomatoes, spinach, and feta cheese!

I highly encourage you to experiment with this pizza. Switch up the kalamata olives for green olives and the spinach for kale, for example.

---

1 ball dough of your choice, at room temperature

2 tablespoons Homemade Pizza Sauce (page 45) or Basil Pesto (page 54)

1 cup packed baby spinach

¼ cup oil-packed sun-dried tomatoes, drained and chopped

10 pitted kalamata olives, halved

1 cup (4 ounces) low-moisture part-skim shredded mozzarella cheese

¼ cup crumbled feta cheese

¼ teaspoon dried oregano

⅛ teaspoon black pepper

Place pizza stone on lowest rack in the oven or, if using a steel, place on the highest rack. Preheat oven to 500°F at least 45 minutes to 1 hour before baking.

Sprinkle a bit of fine cornmeal and all-purpose flour on a pizza peel or piece of parchment. Stretch out the dough and shape into a circle (see page 22), then transfer to prepared peel or parchment. Spread pizza sauce over dough leaving a 1-inch border around the edge, then top with spinach, sun-dried tomatoes and olives. Sprinkle mozzarella and feta cheese over the top, then garnish with oregano and black pepper.

Bake until the cheese is melted and the crust is golden, 8–10 minutes.

Remove the pizza from the oven and transfer to a cutting board. Cut into slices and enjoy immediately.

WINE PAIRING: Cannonball's Merlot

Simple Margarita

MAKES: ONE 10-INCH PIZZA

I like to garnish this pizza with basil after baking and slicing, because it keeps the basil green and fresh. But there's nothing wrong with adding it before you cook the pizza. Try it both ways and see which one you prefer!

---

1 ball dough of your choice, at room temperature

1 tablespoon extra-virgin olive oil

¼ cup Crushed Tomato & Basil Sauce (page 56)

4 ounces fresh mozzarella, sliced

1 cup fresh basil, torn

Flaky sea salt and black pepper

Place pizza stone on lowest rack in the oven or, if using a steel, place on the highest rack. Preheat oven to 500°F at least 45 minutes to 1 hour before baking.

Sprinkle a bit of fine cornmeal and all-purpose flour on a pizza peel or piece of parchment. Stretch out the dough and shape into a circle (see page 22), then transfer to prepared peel or parchment. Brush top of dough with olive oil, then spread sauce over dough leaving a 1-inch border around the edge. Top with mozzarella slices.

Bake until the cheese is melted and the crust is golden, 8–10 minutes.

Remove the pizza from the oven and transfer it to a cutting board. Garnish with basil, sea salt and black pepper. Cut into slices and enjoy immediately.

Roasted Tomato Margarita

MAKES: ONE 10-INCH PIZZA

Talk about flavor! *Have you ever roasted cherry tomatoes? If you haven't, now is the time! When tossed with oil, salt and black pepper and roasted, they pop open, caramelize, and become super sweet. They are one of the most perfect toppings for pizza! It's important to know that this pizza can be a bit heavy. Because of that, I usually bake it on parchment so that I can easily transfer it to and out of the oven.*

1 pint cherry tomatoes, washed and dried

3 tablespoons extra-virgin olive oil

2 cloves garlic

¼ teaspoon kosher salt

¼ teaspoon black pepper, divided

1 ball dough of your choice, at room temperature

4 ounces fresh mozzarella, sliced

1 cup fresh basil, torn

Place pizza stone on lowest rack in the oven or, if using a steel, place on the highest rack. Preheat oven to 500°F at least 45 minutes to 1 hour before baking.

Toss the tomatoes with the olive oil, garlic, salt and ⅛ teaspoon black pepper. Spread tomatoes out onto a foil-lined baking sheet and place on top oven rack. While the oven is preheating, bake the tomatoes, stirring once halfway through cooking, until tomatoes are blistered and juicy, 15–20 minutes. Note: Keep your eye on these tomatoes since they'll be cooking in the oven as it's preheating.

Sprinkle a bit of fine cornmeal and all-purpose flour on a pizza peel or piece of parchment. Stretch out the dough, shape into a circle (see page 22) and transfer to prepared peel or parchment. Top stretched dough with roasted tomato mixture and cover with mozzarella slices. Sprinkle on top with the remaining ⅛ teaspoon black pepper.

Bake until the cheese is melted and the crust is golden, 8–10 minutes.

Remove the pizza from the oven and transfer it to a cutting board. Garnish with basil, cut into slices and enjoy immediately.

WINE PAIRING: Cakebread Cellars' Apple Barn Pinot Noir

Spinach, Hearts of Palm & Feta

MAKES: ONE 10-INCH PIZZA

I'm guilty of putting spinach on pizza 95 percent of the time. For some reason, I always feel like it's the perfect ingredient. It's light, it's pretty, and it pairs well with so many other ingredients. So, embrace it and join the "spinach-on-everything" club!

Hearts of palm can usually be found in the aisle with jarred condiments or canned vegetables. If your store doesn't have them, substitute with equal amounts of chopped, marinated artichoke hearts.

---

1 ball dough of your choice, at room temperature

2 tablespoons Roasted Red Pepper Sauce (page 49)

1 cup packed baby spinach

½ cup sliced hearts of palm, rinsed

1 cup low-moisture part-skim shredded mozzarella cheese (4 ounces)

¼ cup crumbled feta cheese

¼ teaspoon dried oregano leaves

⅛ teaspoon black pepper

Place your pizza stone on the lowest rack in the oven or, if using a steel, place on the highest rack. Preheat oven to 500°F at least 45 minutes to 1 hour before baking.

Sprinkle a bit of fine cornmeal and all-purpose flour on a pizza peel or piece of parchment. Stretch out the dough and shape into a circle (see page 22), then transfer to prepared peel or parchment. Spread red pepper sauce over dough leaving a 1-inch border around the edge, then top with spinach and hearts of palm. Sprinkle mozzarella and feta cheese on top and garnish with oregano and black pepper.

Bake until the cheese is melted and the crust is golden, 8–10 minutes.

Remove the pizza from the oven and transfer it to a cutting board. Cut into slices and enjoy immediately.

WINE PAIRING: Melville Estate's Pinot Noir

Roasted Mushroom & Goat Cheese

MAKES: ONE 10-INCH PIZZA

You'll notice that I like to roast stuff. Like a lot. That's because first, it's an easy, no-fuss cooking method and second, it creates such flavorful food. These mushrooms are proof of that! Toss them with oil and some shallots and roast, and you've created pure kitchen magic!

Use any variety of mushroom you like for this recipe—they're all delicious, so you can't go wrong. One tip: be sure to cut mushrooms so that they're all about the same size to ensure they roast evenly.

---

12 ounces mixed mushrooms (Portobello, cremini, shiitake, or other), cut into bite-size pieces

3 tablespoons extra-virgin olive oil, divided

¼ teaspoon kosher salt

⅛ teaspoon black pepper

2 shallots, cut into ½-inch thick slices

1 ball dough of your choice, at room temperature

2 tablespoons Homemade Pizza Sauce (page 45)

1 cup low-moisture part-skim shredded mozzarella cheese (4 ounces)

¼ cup crumbled goat cheese

Flaky sea salt

1 teaspoon chopped fresh thyme

2 tablespoons Balsamic Reduction (page 176)

Position one oven rack at the highest setting. Place pizza stone on lowest rack in the oven or, if using a steel, place on the highest rack. Preheat oven to 500°F at least 45 minutes to 1 hour before baking. Place a baking sheet on the highest rack while oven preheats.

Cook the mushrooms while the oven preheats: Toss mushrooms with 2 tablespoons oil, salt, and black pepper. Carefully remove preheated baking sheet from the oven and add the mushrooms, spreading them out in an even layer. Return the baking sheet to the upper rack and roast for 8 minutes.

Meanwhile, toss the shallots with the remaining 1 tablespoon oil. Remove baking sheet and add the shallot; give everything a stir, then return baking sheet to oven and roast, stirring once halfway, until mushrooms are golden, 8 minutes.

Shape the dough. Sprinkle a bit of fine cornmeal and all-purpose flour on a pizza peel or piece of parchment. Stretch out the dough and shape into a circle (see page 22), then transfer to prepared peel or parchment. Spread pizza sauce over dough leaving a 1-inch border around the edge, then top with roasted mushrooms and shallots. Sprinkle mozzarella and goat cheese over the top.

Bake until the crust is golden and the cheese is bubbly, about 8–10 minutes.

Remove pizza from the oven and transfer it to a cutting board. Garnish with sea salt, thyme, and drizzle with balsamic reduction. Cut into slices and enjoy immediately.

WINE PAIRING: Melville Sandy's Block Pinot Noir

Asparagus & Pistachio

MAKES: ONE 10-INCH PIZZA

I love adding a bit of unexpected crunch to foods, and pizza is no exception. Pistachios pair so well with asparagus and goat cheese, so they were a no-brainer when it came to making this pizza.

I like the subtle sweetness and slight nuttiness of sherry vinegar, but if you don't have any, it can easily be replaced with any other acid, including lemon juice!

---

1 ball dough of your choice, at room temperature

2 tablespoons Homemade Pizza Sauce (page 45)

1 cup baby spinach

4 ounces thin asparagus, trimmed and cut diagonally into 1-inch pieces (about ¾ cup cut)

4 ounces fresh mozzarella, sliced

¼ cup crumbled goat cheese

¼ cup lightly salted pistachios, roughly chopped

1 teaspoon sherry vinegar

Garnishes:
crushed red pepper (optional), flaky sea salt, black pepper

Place pizza stone on the lowest rack in the oven or, if using a steel, place on the highest rack. Preheat oven to 500°F at least 45 minutes to 1 hour before baking.

Sprinkle a bit of fine cornmeal and all-purpose flour on a pizza peel or piece of parchment. Stretch out the dough and shape into a circle (see page 22), then transfer to prepared peel or parchment. Spread pizza sauce over dough leaving a 1-inch border around the edge, then top with spinach and asparagus. Cover with mozzarella and goat cheese.

Bake until the cheese is melted and the crust is golden, 8–10 minutes.

Remove pizza from the oven and transfer it to a cutting board. Top with pistachios and drizzle with sherry vinegar. Garnish with crushed red pepper (if using), sea salt and black pepper. Cut into slices and enjoy immediately.

RECIPE NOTE: If you like, place asparagus on top of the cheese instead of under it. You'll get a more roasted effect on it that way.

Ricotta, Balsamic Onions & Pecans

MAKES: ONE 10-INCH PIZZA

If fall were a pizza, it would be this pizza! Sweet potatoes and shallots are roasted to golden perfection before they're added. A few dollops of ricotta brings it all together along with that finishing touch of toasted pecans!

You can buy pre-made balsamic reduction or "syrup" at the store, but making it is easy. See page 176 to make your own! You can easily whip up a batch while you're cooking the onions for this pizza.

---

1 sweet yellow onion, thinly sliced

1 tablespoon extra-virgin olive oil

3 tablespoons balsamic vinegar, divided

1 teaspoon granulated sugar

¼ teaspoon kosher salt

⅛ teaspoon black pepper

1 ball dough of your choice, at room temperature

2 tablespoons **Basil Pesto** (page 54)

½ cup full-fat or part-skim ricotta cheese

½ cup low-moisture part-skim shredded mozzarella cheese (2 ounces)

½ cup pecan halves, toasted

1 tablespoon chopped, fresh oregano or ¼ teaspoon dried oregano

Flaky sea salt, for garnishing

2 tablespoons **Balsamic Reduction** (page 176)

Preheat the oven to 400°F. Place a small, rimmed baking sheet covered with foil on the middle rack in the oven while it preheats. Place another rack on either the top rack, if using a steel, or the bottom rack, if using a stone. Add your stone or steel accordingly.

Toss the onion with olive oil, 2 tablespoons of balsamic vinegar, sugar, ¼ teaspoon salt and black pepper. Carefully remove baking sheet from the oven, add the onions, cover with another piece of foil, and roast 20 minutes, stirring halfway through cooking time. Remove the pan from the oven, uncover and add the remaining 1 tablespoon of vinegar; stir, leave uncovered and return to oven. Roast until golden and tender, about 10–15 minutes. Remove from oven and set aside.

Increase heat to 500°F.

Sprinkle a bit of fine cornmeal and all-purpose flour on a pizza peel or piece of parchment. Stretch out the dough and shape into a circle (see page 22), then transfer to prepared peel or parchment. Spread pesto over dough leaving a 1-inch border around the edge, then top with caramelized onions. Drop dollops of ricotta cheese over onions, then sprinkle mozzarella on top.

Bake until the crust is golden and the cheese is bubbly, 8–10 minutes.

Remove the pizza from the oven and transfer it to a cutting board. Garnish with pecans, oregano, and flaky sea salt. Drizzle with balsamic reduction. Cut into slices and enjoy immediately.

WINE PAIRING: Cannonball's Cabernet Sauvignon

Giardiniera & Spinach

MAKES: ONE 10-INCH PIZZA

I didn't know a thing about giardiniera until I moved to Chicago. Once I sampled it, I was hooked. It's a spicy Italian condiment that tastes good on just about anything, including pizza.

---

1 ball dough of your choice, at room temperature

2 tablespoons extra-virgin olive oil

½ teaspoon Italian seasoning

1 clove garlic, finely minced

1 cup packed baby spinach

½ cup thinly sliced red bell pepper (from 1 pepper)

¼ cup thinly sliced red onion (from 1 onion)

2 tablespoons giardiniera or pickled vegetables

2 (1-ounce) slices Provolone cheese

1 tablespoon chopped fresh parsley

Black pepper, for garnishing

Place the pizza stone on the lowest rack in the oven or, if using a steel, place on the highest rack. Preheat oven to 500°F at least 45 minutes to 1 hour before baking.

Sprinkle a bit of fine cornmeal and all-purpose flour on a pizza peel or piece of parchment. Stretch out the dough and shape into a circle (see page 22), then transfer to prepared peel or parchment. Combine oil, Italian seasoning and garlic together in a small bowl; spread over dough, leaving a 1-inch border around the edge. Top with spinach, bell pepper, onion and giardiniera. Tear provolone slices and lay on top.

Bake until the cheese is melted and the crust is golden, 8–10 minutes.

Remove pizza from the oven and transfer it to a cutting board. Garnish with black pepper, cut into slices and enjoy immediately.

WINE PAIRING: Cakebread Cellars' Sauvignon Blanc

Olive Tapenade

MAKES: ONE 10-INCH PIZZA

Back in college I worked as a prep chef in a nice restaurant. One of my jobs was to make olive tapenade. I had no idea what that was, but soon learned that it was pretty special stuff. I loved it and often took a tiny bit home to enjoy on my flavorless frozen pizzas. Here's my ode to that pizza.

1 ball dough of your choice, at room temperature

2 tablespoons Olive & Sun-Dried Tomato Tapenade (page 50)

1 cup packed baby spinach

¼ cup thinly sliced red onion

4 ounces fresh mozzarella, sliced

¼ cup crumbled feta cheese

Black pepper, for garnishing

1 tablespoon finely chopped parsley

Place pizza stone on lowest rack in the oven or, if using a steel, place on the highest rack. Preheat oven to 500°F at least 45 minutes to 1 hour before baking.

Sprinkle a bit of fine cornmeal and all-purpose flour on a pizza peel or piece of parchment. Stretch out the dough and shape into a circle (see page 22), then transfer to prepared peel or parchment. Spread tapenade over dough leaving a 1-inch border around the edge, then top with spinach and onion. Cover with mozzarella slices and feta cheese.

Bake until the cheese is melted and crust is golden, 8–10 minutes.

Remove the pizza from the oven and transfer it to a cutting board. Garnish with black pepper and parsley. Cut into slices and enjoy immediately.

Asparagus, Artichoke Hearts & Capers

MAKES: ONE 10-INCH PIZZA

When asparagus is in-season, I'm always looking for ways to work it into my recipes, including pizza. For this recipe I prefer thin asparagus spears so that they cook quickly and evenly. But if you can only find thicker spears, no problem, just slice them in half lengthwise!

---

1 ball dough of your choice, at room temperature

2 tablespoons Crushed Tomato & Basil Sauce (page 56)

4 ounces thin asparagus, trimmed and cut diagonally into 1-inch pieces (about ¾ cup cut)

½ cup canned quartered artichoke hearts packed in water, drained and roughly chopped

1 tablespoon capers, rinsed and chopped

½ cup low-moisture part-skim shredded mozzarella cheese (2 ounces)

¼ cup shredded asiago or Parmesan cheese (1 ounce)

¼ teaspoon black pepper

¼ teaspoon cracked red pepper

Flaky sea salt, for garnishing

Place pizza stone on lowest rack in the oven or, if using a steel, place on the highest rack. Preheat oven to 500°F at least 45 minutes to 1 hour before baking.

Sprinkle a bit of fine cornmeal and all-purpose flour on a pizza peel or piece of parchment. Stretch out the dough and shape into a circle (see page 22), then transfer to prepared peel or parchment. Spread tomato and basil sauce over dough leaving a 1-inch border around the edge, then top with asparagus, artichoke hearts and capers. Sprinkle mozzarella and asiago cheese on top.

Bake until the cheese is melted and the crust is golden, 8–10 minutes.

Remove pizza from the oven and transfer it to a cutting board. Garnish with black pepper, cracked red pepper and flaky sea salt. Cut into slices and enjoy immediately.

SPECIAL NOTE: You can typically build a pizza on a pizza peel, but for this recipe, I definitely recommend using parchment. That's because the toppings make it a bit heavy, which can make it hard to transfer from peel to oven. Save yourself the frustration and pull out the parchment for this one.

Hominy, Poblano & Cilantro

MAKES: ONE 10-INCH PIZZA

Do these ingredients belong on a pizza? Of course they do! I've been smitten with hominy ever since I met my first bowl of posole. Since then, I've been trying to find unique ways to sneak it into other recipes. I love the subtle corn flavor it provides, which pairs so nicely with the roasted poblano and fresh cilantro.

1 poblano pepper

½ cup canned hominy, rinsed and patted dry

1 teaspoon extra-virgin olive oil

¼ teaspoon ground cumin

¼ teaspoon chili powder

⅛ teaspoon kosher salt

1 ball dough of your choice, at room temperature

2 tablespoons Fire-Roasted Tomato Salsa (page 61) plus extra for serving

½ cup (2 ounces) shredded sharp cheddar cheese

½ cup (2 ounces) low-moisture part-skim shredded mozzarella cheese

1 cup fresh cilantro, torn

1 green onion, thinly sliced on the bias

2 teaspoons fresh lime juice (from 1 lime)

1 ripe avocado, diced

Flaky sea salt, for garnishing

Place pizza stone on lowest rack in the oven or, if using a steel, place on the highest rack. Preheat oven to 425°F.

Toss hominy with oil, cumin, chili powder and salt. Spread out onto foil-lined baking sheet and roast on top rack for 20 minutes. Remove from the oven and set aside.

Increase oven temperature to 500°F.

While the oven preheats, roast the poblano. Using metal tongs, hold the pepper directly over a gas flame or under a broiler, and turn regularly until blistered and blackened all over, about 5 (direct flame) to 10 minutes (broiler). Transfer pepper to a bowl and cover with plastic wrap or towel until cool enough to handle. Remove from bowl and rub off any of the blackened skin as well as the stem and seeds, discard. Rinse pepper under cool water and slice into strips.

Sprinkle a bit of fine cornmeal and all-purpose flour on a pizza peel or piece of parchment. Stretch out the dough and shape into a circle (see page 22), then transfer to prepared peel or parchment. Spread 2 tablespoons salsa over dough leaving a 1-inch border around the edge, then top with poblano and hominy. Sprinkle cheddar and mozzarella cheese on top.

Bake until the cheese is melted and the crust is golden, 8–10 minutes.

Remove pizza from the oven and transfer it to a cutting board. Garnish with cilantro, green onion, lime juice and avocado. Top with a little flaky sea salt, then cut into slices and enjoy immediately. Serve extra salsa on the side.

INGREDIENT NOTE: If you can't find poblano peppers or hominy at your grocery store, try your local Mexican grocery store or online grocer.

BBQ Kale

MAKES: ONE 10-INCH PIZZA

I see you rolling your eyes at me, but you had to know I was going to put something with kale in this cookbook. I am a dietitian after all. But guess what, this combo is good! And sure, kale is good for you, but I also love the bite it provides, and that sweet BBQ sauce is a nice pairing to that earthy, kale vibe.

Any type of kale will work on this pizza, so if you can't find dinosaur, just use curly kale instead. In more good news, just about any green will work here too. Experiment with them all!

---

1 ball dough of your choice, at room temperature

2 tablespoons Easy BBQ Sauce (page 57)

2 cups stemmed, shredded kale, preferably dinosaur or lacinato

¼ cup thinly sliced red onion

½ cup (2 ounces) low-moisture part-skim shredded mozzarella cheese

½ cup (2 ounces) shredded sharp cheddar cheese

½ green apple, sliced into thin sticks, julienned

1 teaspoon crushed red pepper

Hot sauce, for serving

Place pizza stone on lowest rack in the oven or, if using a steel, place on the highest rack. Preheat oven to 500°F at least 45 minutes to 1 hour before baking.

Sprinkle a bit of fine cornmeal and all-purpose flour on a pizza peel or piece of parchment. Stretch out the dough and shape into a circle (see page 22), then transfer to prepared peel or parchment. Spread BBQ sauce over dough leaving a 1-inch border around the edge, then top with kale and onion. Sprinkle mozzarella and cheddar cheese on top.

Bake until the cheese is melted and the crust is golden, 8–10 minutes.

Remove the pizza from the oven and transfer it to a cutting board. Garnish with apple and crushed red pepper, then cut into slices and enjoy immediately. Serve hot sauce on the side.

COOKING NOTE: You'll have a rather large pile of kale on this pizza before you cook it. That's okay! You're doing it right! It'll cook down in the oven!

Peach & Jalapeño

MAKES: ONE 10-INCH PIZZA

Once upon a time, I had peach BBQ-sauce-covered chicken and thought, "Why didn't I think of that?" This pizza is kind of like that chicken, a hit of spicy paired with a hit of sweetness. It's a flavor combination that's pretty darn tasty.

If your peaches seem a bit wet, pat them dry before adding to the pizza. Remember, water as a topping is no good; it'll just result in soggy pizza.

If it's not peach season where you live, substitute fresh peaches with ½ cup canned or frozen peaches. If you want to use canned, I recommend purchasing peaches packed in 100 percent juice. Drain them, then pat dry before chopping and adding to this pizza. If you want to use frozen peaches, allow them to thaw completely. Then, pat dry and chop before adding to the pizza.

---

1 ball dough of your choice, at room temperature

2 tablespoons Easy BBQ Sauce (page 57)

1 cup low-moisture part-skim shredded mozzarella cheese (4 ounces)

¼ cup crumbled feta cheese

1 small ripe peach, diced small (about ½ cup diced)

¼ cup diced red onion

½ jalapeño, diced

¼ cup fresh cilantro, chopped

½ teaspoon lime zest plus 1 tablespoon lime juice (from 1 lime)

¼ teaspoon kosher salt

Place pizza stone on lowest rack in the oven or, if using a steel, place on the highest rack. Preheat oven to 500°F at least 45 minutes to 1 hour before baking.

Sprinkle a bit of fine cornmeal and all-purpose flour on a pizza peel or piece of parchment. Stretch out the dough and shape into a circle (see page 22), then transfer to prepared peel or parchment. Spread BBQ sauce over dough leaving a 1-inch border around the edge, then sprinkle mozzarella and feta cheese on top.

Bake until the cheese is melted and the crust is golden, 8–10 minutes.

While pizza is baking, toss the peaches with the red onion, jalapeño, cilantro, lime zest, lime juice and salt.

Remove pizza from the oven and transfer it to a cutting board. Garnish with peach salsa, then cut into slices and enjoy immediately.

Capers, Sun-Dried Tomatoes & Basil

MAKES: ONE 10-INCH PIZZA

Great news! This pizza comes together fast, especially if you grab a store-bought pesto or if you've made a big batch of the pesto from this book. Here's a hint: you can store it in the freezer for moments just like this! It's perfect for a quick dinner.

1 ball dough of your choice, at room temperature

2 tablespoons Basil Pesto (page 54)

1 cup packed baby spinach

⅓ cup slivered oil–packed sun–dried tomatoes, drained

2 teaspoons capers, rinsed and chopped

4 ounces fresh mozzarella cheese, thinly sliced

1 cup fresh basil, torn

Place pizza stone on lowest rack in the oven or, if using a steel, place on the highest rack. Preheat oven to 500°F at least 45 minutes to 1 hour before baking.

Sprinkle a bit of fine cornmeal and all-purpose flour on a pizza peel or piece of parchment. Stretch out the dough and shape into a circle (see page 22). Transfer to prepared peel or parchment. Spread pesto over dough leaving a 1-inch border around the edge, then top with spinach, sun-dried tomatoes and capers. Sprinkle cheese on top.

Bake until the cheese is melted and the crust is golden, 8–10 minutes.

Remove pizza from the oven and transfer it to a cutting board. Garnish with basil, cut into slices and enjoy immediately.

INGREDIENT NOTE: If you have extra basil leaves, store them like a pro! Simply wrap (unwashed!) in clean paper towels and place back in the original container or a resealable storage bag. If your basil is fresh from the garden or farmer's market (usually these will have longer stems, like flowers), trim the ends and place in a glass with water. Cover with some plastic wrap and refrigerate. Change the water every other day to keep it fresh.

Pistachio Chimichurri & Ricotta

MAKES: ONE 10-INCH PIZZA

When I made this chimichurri, I dreamt of the numerous ways I could use it. I love this simple version that packs so much flavor! It pairs especially well with the creamy ricotta cheese. Definitely a pairing you don't want to miss!

---

1 ball dough of your choice, at room temperature

¼ cup **Pistachio Chimichurri (page 53)**

1 cup packed baby spinach, thinly sliced

1 cup low-moisture, full-fat or part-skim shredded mozzarella cheese (4 ounces)

¼ cup ricotta cheese

1 cup cherry or grape tomatoes, halved

Flaky sea salt, for garnishing

Place pizza stone on lowest rack in the oven or, if using a steel, place on the highest rack. Preheat oven to 500°F at least 45 minutes to 1 hour before baking.

Sprinkle a bit of fine cornmeal and all-purpose flour on a pizza peel or piece of parchment. Stretch out the dough and shape into a circle (see page 22), then transfer to prepared peel or parchment. Spread chimichurri over dough leaving a 1-inch border around the edge, then top with spinach. Sprinkle mozzarella cheese on top and add dollops of ricotta cheese. Top with cherry tomatoes, cut sides facing up.

Bake until the cheese is melted and the crust is golden, 8–10 minutes.

Remove pizza from the oven and transfer it to a cutting board. Garnish with sea salt. Cut into slices and enjoy immediately.

WINE PAIRING: Cakebread Cellars' Sauvignon Blanc

Brussels Sprouts & Pecorino

MAKES: ONE 10-INCH PIZZA

Growing up, I strongly disliked Brussels sprouts. My mom would buy them frozen and then "steam" them in the microwave. They looked so sad after that and smelled even worse. Sorry mom! But now that I'm older (and also a parent), I realize the beauty of Brussels sprouts. I love them thinly sliced and paired with a bit of salty cheese. I enjoy them raw or roasted, but definitely NOT cooked in the microwave.

1 tablespoon avocado or canola oil

1 cup thinly sliced Brussels sprouts

¼ teaspoon kosher salt

⅛ teaspoon black pepper, plus extra for garnish

1 clove garlic, minced

1 ball dough of your choice, at room temperature

2 tablespoons Sara's Buttermilk Ranch (page 62)

1¼ cups finely grated Pecorino Romano cheese

1 teaspoon lemon zest plus 2 teaspoons lemon juice (from 1 lemon)

Place pizza stone on lowest rack in the oven or, if using a steel, place on the highest rack. Preheat oven to 500°F at least 45 minutes to 1 hour before baking.

Heat the oil in a wok or stainless steel skillet (preferably one with slanted sides) over high heat. Add Brussels sprouts, salt, and black pepper, and cook, stirring frequently, until just bright green and charred in spots, about 4 minutes. Remove from heat, add garlic, and cook off the heat until fragrant, 1 minute. Set aside.

Sprinkle a bit of fine cornmeal and all-purpose flour on a pizza peel or piece of parchment. Stretch out the dough and shape into a circle (see page 22), then transfer to prepared peel or parchment. Spread Buttermilk Ranch over dough leaving a 1-inch border around the edge, then top with Brussels sprouts and scatter cheese over the top.

Bake until the cheese is melted and the crust is golden, 8–10 minutes.

Remove the pizza from the oven and transfer it to a cutting board. Garnish with lemon zest and lemon juice, cut into slices and enjoy immediately.

Pesto, Spinach & Basil Goat Cheese

MAKES: ONE 10-INCH PIZZA

The first time I encountered pesto was on a pizza. Go figure. But that first introduction started an intense love of this fabulous Italian sauce. It makes a great base to this pizza and pairs nicely with Basil Goat Cheese and fresh tomatoes.

---

1 ball dough of your choice, at room temperature

2 tablespoons Basil Pesto (page 54)

1 cup packed baby spinach

1 cup low-moisture part-skim shredded mozzarella cheese (4 ounces)

¼ cup Basil Goat Cheese (page 108)

10 cherry tomatoes, halved lengthwise

1 cup fresh basil, torn

Flaky sea salt and black pepper, for garnishing

Place pizza stone on lowest rack in the oven or, if using a steel, place on the highest rack. Preheat oven to 500°F at least 45 minutes to 1 hour before baking.

Sprinkle a bit of fine cornmeal and all-purpose flour on a pizza peel or piece of parchment. Stretch out the dough and shape into a circle (see page 22), then transfer to prepared peel or parchment. Spread pesto over dough leaving a 1-inch border around the edge. Top with spinach, then cover with mozzarella cheese. Add dollops of Basil Goat Cheese, then cherry tomatoes, cut sides facing up.

Bake until the cheese is melted and the crust is golden, 8–10 minutes.

Remove the pizza from the oven and transfer it to a cutting board. Garnish with fresh basil, flaky sea salt and black pepper. Cut into slices and enjoy immediately.

INGREDIENT NOTE: Interested in trying another green here? Baby kale or arugula would be a delicious option.

Hummus & Roasted Red Pepper

MAKES: ONE 10-INCH PIZZA

One night I was making pizza and realized I was out of pizza sauce. As it turned out, I was also out of just about anything to make a sauce. UNTIL, I found the hummus and thought, "That would be good on pizza, wouldn't it?" Even though I wasn't 100 percent sure, I went for it and was pleasantly surprised. Spoiler alert! Hummus IS good on pizza!

If you don't have time to whip up a batch of homemade hummus, that's okay. Any store-bought variety of hummus will work here. I personally love lemon and roasted red pepper but have fun and experiment!

---

1 ball dough of your choice, at room temperature

¼ cup Hummus (page 58)

1 cup packed baby spinach

1 jarred roasted red bell pepper, thinly sliced

1 cup low-moisture part-skim shredded mozzarella cheese (4 ounces)

¼ cup crumbled feta cheese

¼ teaspoon smoked paprika

1 tablespoon finely chopped curly parsley

Flaky sea salt and black pepper, for garnishing

Place pizza stone on lowest rack in the oven or, if using a steel, place on the highest rack. Preheat oven to 500°F at least 45 minutes to 1 hour before baking.

Sprinkle a bit of fine cornmeal and all-purpose flour on a pizza peel or piece of parchment. Stretch out the dough and shape into a circle (see page 22), then transfer to prepared peel or parchment. Spread hummus over dough leaving a 1-inch border around the edge, then top with spinach and bell pepper. Sprinkle mozzarella and feta cheese, then sprinkle with smoked paprika.

Bake until the cheese is melted and the crust is golden, 8–10 minutes.

Remove the pizza from the oven and transfer it to a cutting board. Garnish with parsley, flaky sea salt and black pepper, then cut into slices and enjoy immediately.

INGREDIENT NOTE: Want a little crunch? Add some chopped walnuts or pine nuts before serving.

Green Olive & Chimichurri

MAKES: ONE 10-INCH PIZZA

I'm all about experimenting, especially when it comes to cooking. That attitude naturally extends to pizza toppings. I love this combination of briny olives with the earthy herbs of chimichurri. It's a beautiful pizza that you will want on repeat.

I love Castelvetrano olives for this pizza because of their firmness and extra bite, but any olive will work here. Just be sure to choose pitted olives or pit them before adding to your pizza.

---

1 ball dough of your choice, at room temperature

2 tablespoons Pistachio Chimichurri (page 53)

1 cup packed baby spinach

10 pitted green olives, roughly chopped

4 ounces fresh mozzarella, sliced

⅛ teaspoon black pepper

1 teaspoon finely chopped parsley

Place pizza stone on lowest rack in the oven or, if using a steel, place on the highest rack. Preheat oven to 500°F at least 45 minutes to 1 hour before baking.

Sprinkle a bit of fine cornmeal and all-purpose flour on a pizza peel or piece of parchment. Stretch out the dough and shape into a circle (see page 22), then transfer to prepared peel or parchment. Spread chimichurri over dough leaving a 1-inch border around the edge, then top with spinach and green olives. Cover with mozzarella cheese slices.

Bake until the cheese is melted and the crust is golden, 8–10 minutes.

Remove the pizza from the oven and transfer it to a cutting board. Garnish with fresh black pepper and parsley. Cut into slices and enjoy immediately.

Double-Dough Pan Pizza

MAKES: ONE 10-INCH PAN PIZZA

Even though I live in Chicago, I actually don't love Chicago-style pizza. I know! I feel bad even writing that, but it's true. For me, it's just too much cheese and sauce. However, I do love a good pan pizza. It's pretty magical to eat a pizza that has such thick, delicious dough! I love this recipe because you can make it in your cast iron pan, which means it's easy to put in and take out of the oven.

A word to the wise: keep an eye on the pizza as it cooks. After 10 minutes of baking, check to see if the bottom appears to be done before the top. A silicone spatula is a good tool for this. If the bottom looks deep brown, transfer it to the top rack of the oven and broil to finish melting the cheese.

1½ tablespoons extra-virgin olive oil

1 batch (2 balls) dough (from any above recipe except gluten-free), at room temperature

¼ cup Homemade Pizza Sauce (page 45)

1½ cups low-moisture part-skim shredded mozzarella cheese (6 ounces)

½ teaspoon dried oregano leaves or Italian seasoning

Optional toppings:
½ cup chopped veggies and/or protein of your choice

Special equipment:
10-inch cast iron skillet

Position one rack to the lowest setting in oven and the other at the top position. Preheat oven to 500°F at least 45 minutes to 1 hour before baking.

Add olive oil to a 10-inch cast iron pan and use clean hands to evenly coat the sides and bottom. Add dough and push gently to fill the pan. If you're met with resistance, cover and rest for 15 minutes and push outward again. Cover with a clean towel and let rise until puffy, about 1 hour.

Sprinkle half of the cheese over the dough, then top with dollops of pizza sauce. Add other toppings, if using. Sprinkle remaining cheese on top and dust with oregano.

Bake until the crust is golden brown and the cheese is melted, about 15–20 minutes.

Remove from the oven. Slide a thin, flexible spatula around the edge to release any "stuck" crust from the side. Transfer to a cooling rack and let rest for 10 minutes before transferring to a cutting board and slicing.

Thin Crust

MAKES: TWO THIN CRUST PIZZAS

If thin crust pizza is what you love, then this recipe is for you! Use it as a guide for transforming any of the pizzas in this book into a thinner version. Just remember, 1 ball of dough will make enough dough for TWO thin crust pizzas and each pizza recipe will make TWO thin crust pizzas.

---

1 ball dough of your choice, at room temperature (from any recipe except gluten-free)

¼ cup Homemade Pizza Sauce (page 45)

1½ cups low-moisture part-skim shredded mozzarella cheese (6 ounces)

½ teaspoon dried oregano leaves or Italian seasoning

Optional toppings:
½ cup chopped veggies and/or protein of your choice

Place pizza stone on lowest rack in the oven or, if using a steel, place on the highest rack. Preheat oven to 500°F at least 45 minutes to 1 hour before baking.

Divide the dough in half. Sprinkle a bit of fine cornmeal and all-purpose flour on a pizza peel or piece of parchment. Use a rolling pin to roll each ball of dough out into a ⅛-inch thick circle. Transfer each pizza to a prepared peel or parchment. Spread some sauce over each pizza leaving a 1-inch border around the edge, then add desired toppings. Sprinkle cheese on top.

Bake until the cheese is melted and the crust is golden, 8–10 minutes.

Remove pizza from the oven and transfer it to a cutting board. Cut into slices and enjoy immediately.

Specialty Pizza

120 Hot Hawaiian

122 Grilled Pesto Chicken

123 Potato & Sausage

124 Hungry Artist

127 Sausage, Fennel & Fontina

128 Spicy Shrimp

131 Prosciutto, Olives &
Red Onion

132 Mushroom & (Some) Sausage

135 Chorizo & Corn

136 BBQ Chicken

138 Ras El Hanout

139 Chicken Giardiniera

141 Breakfast Pizza

142 Pulled Pork & Cabbage Slaw

143 Baked Potato

Hot Hawaiian

MAKES: ONE 10-INCH PIZZA

As a kid, I typically ate cheese pizza. Not because I liked it all that much, but because it's what was usually offered to me. As if I had no taste buds! Then, one day, I got my hands on a slice of Hawaiian-style pizza and I was hooked. And I still am! I love this combo so much—that sweet pineapple paired with salty ham—YUM! My adult version comes with a little extra heat in the form of jalapeños and pepperoncini. If the heat is too much for you, just leave those additions off! Topping order matters! If you like your ham a little crispy, place it on top of the cheese before baking. If you can't find fresh pineapple, substitute with canned or even thawed, frozen pineapple. Remember to drain and pat dry before adding to your pizza.

---

1 ball dough of your choice, at room temperature

2 tablespoons Easy BBQ Sauce (page 57)

1 cup baby spinach

½ cup fresh or canned pineapple chunks, cut into thin slices

¼ cup thinly sliced jalapeño

¼ cup jarred sliced pepperoncini peppers, drained

1 cup low-moisture part-skim shredded mozzarella cheese (4 ounces)

4 ounces Canadian bacon or ham, sliced into strips or squares

Crushed red pepper, for garnishing (optional)

Place pizza stone on lowest rack in the oven or, if using a steel, place on the highest rack. Preheat oven to 500°F at least 45 minutes to 1 hour before baking.

Sprinkle a bit of fine cornmeal and all-purpose flour on a pizza peel or piece of parchment. Stretch out the dough and shape into a circle (see page 22), then transfer to prepared peel or parchment. Spread BBQ sauce over dough leaving a 1-inch border around the edge, then top with spinach, pineapple, jalapeño and pepperoncini. Sprinkle cheese over the top, then add the Canadian bacon.

Bake until the cheese is melted and the crust is golden, 8–10 minutes.

Remove pizza from the oven and transfer it to a cutting board. Garnish with crushed red pepper (if using). Cut into slices and enjoy immediately.

INGREDIENT NOTE: If using canned pineapple, I recommend buying pineapple packed in its own juices. The ones packed in syrup will be too sweet for this recipe.

BRIGHT IDEA: If you can find fresh pineapple, I recommend using it for this recipe. For a whole pineapple, peel, core and then cut into paper-thin slices instead of chunks. It looks gorgeous when placed on top of the cheese before baking.

Grilled Pesto Chicken

MAKES: TWO 10-INCH PIZZAS

My Dad is a boss at the grill! Growing up, I remember watching him grill everything from chicken to steak. When he brought it to the table, we all started salivating. While I'll never be as good of a grill master as him, I continuously try. This pizza is dedicated to my grilling hero, Richard Coffman!

Canola or vegetable oil, as needed for grill

1 small red bell pepper, stemmed, seeded and quartered

½ small red onion, cut into ½-inch rounds

1 (6 ounce) boneless, skinless chicken breast, pounded to ¼-inch thickness

¼ teaspoon kosher salt

⅛ teaspoon black pepper

2 balls dough of your choice, at room temperature

1 tablespoon extra-virgin olive oil

2 tablespoons plus ¼ cup Basil Pesto (page 54), divided

1 cup low-moisture part-skim shredded mozzarella cheese (4 ounces)

½ cup fresh basil leaves, torn

Preheat grill to high heat. Clean grill grates, then thoroughly coat with oil. Season peppers, onions and chicken with salt and black pepper. Add chicken to one side of the grill and veggies to the opposite side. Grill chicken and vegetables, turning once, until chicken is just cooked through (internal temperature should reach 165°F) and vegetables just tender, 4–6 minutes total. Transfer chicken and vegetables to a cutting board and let rest for 5 minutes. Thinly slice chicken, chop the veggies and toss everything with 2 tablespoons of the pesto.

Sprinkle a bit of fine cornmeal and all-purpose flour on a pizza peel, parchment or inverted baking sheet. Stretch out and shape both dough balls into a circle (see page 22). Transfer to prepared peel, parchment or baking sheet. Brush the tops with a little olive oil.

Transfer the dough, oiled-side down, from the pizza peel to the grill grates. Close the lid and grill until bottom is lightly browned, about 2 minutes. Using tongs, flip the dough and working quickly, spread the tops with the remaining 2 tablespoons pesto each, then top with chicken, vegetables and cheese. Close the lid and cook until cheese is melted, about 4–5 minutes.

Remove pizzas from the grill and transfer to a cutting board. Garnish with fresh basil, cut into slices and enjoy immediately.

PREP NOTE: Consider dividing the dough into 4 balls. This creates a more individual size pizza. This way you can adjust toppings as needed. Also, a smaller pizza can be easier to work with at the grill.

Potato & Sausage

MAKES: ONE 10-INCH PIZZA

I love the flavors of potatoes and sausage together! That combination just makes me feel warm and cozy. Why not put it on a pizza? Roasting the potatoes first takes some of the "crunch" off of them. I know it's an extra step, but it's worth it.

If you can't find bulk sausage, buy sausage links. Remove sausage from casings and discard them. Then add the sausage to your pizza.

½ pound small red potatoes, quartered then cut into ¼-inch slices

1 tablespoon extra-virgin olive oil

¼ teaspoon kosher salt

⅛ teaspoon black pepper plus extra for garnishing

1 ball dough of your choice, at room temperature

2 tablespoons Homemade Pizza Sauce (page 45)

½ cup shredded fontina cheese (2 ounces)

½ cup shredded mozzarella cheese (2 ounces)

4 ounces bulk mild Italian sausage

1 tablespoon fresh rosemary leaves, chopped (or ¼ teaspoon dried rosemary)

Place pizza stone on lowest rack in the oven or, if using a steel, place on the highest rack. Preheat oven to 400°F.

Line a baking sheet with parchment paper. Toss potatoes with oil, salt, and black pepper. Spread potatoes out in a single layer onto prepared baking sheet. Roast for 30 minutes or until potatoes are lightly browned and centers are tender, stirring once halfway through cooking time. Remove from oven, then increase oven heat to 500°F.

Sprinkle a bit of fine cornmeal and all-purpose flour on a pizza peel or piece of parchment. Stretch out the dough and shape into a circle (see page 22), then transfer to prepared peel or parchment. Spread pizza sauce over the dough leaving a 1-inch border around the edge, then cover with potatoes. Sprinkle fontina and mozzarella cheese over potatoes. Pinch off bite-size pieces of sausage and add to the top.

Bake until cheese is melted and crust is golden, 8–10 minutes.

Remove the pizza from the oven and transfer it to a cutting board. Garnish with basil and black pepper, then cut into slices and enjoy immediately.

Hungry Artist

MAKES: ONE 10-INCH PIZZA

Fun fact! My mom and my daughter are incredibly talented artists! And they both love pepperoni. Go figure. Of course I had to have a pizza dedicated to them. While I'm still trying to convince my daughter that other pizza toppings exist, my mom loves black olives and green peppers with her pepperoni pizza, so I've added them here.

---

1 ball dough of your choice, at room temperature

2 tablespoons Homemade Pizza Sauce (page 45)

4 ounces pepperoni, thinly sliced

½ cup green bell pepper cut into ¼-inch-thick rounds

¼ cup sliced black olives

1 cup low-moisture part-skim shredded mozzarella cheese (4 ounces)

¼ teaspoon Italian seasoning

Place pizza stone on lowest rack in the oven or, if using a steel, place on the highest rack. Preheat oven to 500°F at least 45 minutes to 1 hour before baking.

Sprinkle a bit of fine cornmeal and all-purpose flour on a pizza peel or piece of parchment. Stretch out the dough and shape into a circle (see page 22), then transfer to prepared peel or parchment. Spread pizza sauce over dough leaving a 1-inch border around the edge, then top with pepperoni, green bell pepper and black olives. Sprinkle cheese on top.

Bake until the cheese is melted and the crust is golden, 8–10 minutes.

Remove the pizza from the oven and transfer it to a cutting board. Garnish with Italian seasoning, then cut into slices and enjoy immediately.

WINE PAIRING: A&C's Proprietary Red

Sausage, Fennel & Fontina

MAKES: ONE 10-INCH PIZZA

My brother's favorite pizza growing up was sausage pizza. I found it repulsive. There was something off-putting about those little brown pieces of meat on top of his pizza. I couldn't handle it. Ironically, I too now love sausage pizza, which I'm sure my brother thinks is hilarious. I can say that while he wasn't right about a lot of stuff, he was right about this, especially when you add a little fennel and onion!

1 tablespoon extra-virgin olive oil

1 cup fennel, thinly sliced

½ cup thinly sliced sweet yellow onion

¼ teaspoon kosher salt

⅛ teaspoon black pepper

1 ball dough of your choice, at room temperature

2 tablespoons Homemade Pizza Sauce (page 45)

1 cup low-moisture part-skim shredded mozzarella cheese (4 ounces)

½ cup shredded fontina cheese (2 ounces)

2 ounces bulk sweet or spicy Italian sausage

¼ teaspoon Italian seasoning

Crushed red pepper, for garnishing (optional)

¼ teaspoon Italian seasoning

Place pizza stone on lowest rack in the oven or, if using a steel, place on the highest rack. Preheat oven to 500°F at least 45 minutes to 1 hour before baking.

Heat the oil in a large skillet over medium–high heat. Add the fennel and onion and cook, stirring occasionally, until golden and just softened, about 3–5 minutes. Season with salt and black pepper. Remove from heat and set aside.

Sprinkle a bit of fine cornmeal and all-purpose flour on a pizza peel or piece of parchment. Stretch out the dough and shape into a circle (see page 22), then transfer to prepared peel or parchment. Spread pizza sauce over dough leaving a 1-inch border around the edge, then sprinkle fennel and onion mixture over the top. Sprinkle mozzarella and fontina cheese on top. Pinch sausage into pieces and place on top of cheese. Dust with Italian seasoning and crushed red pepper (if using).

Bake until the cheese is melted and the crust is golden, 8–10 minutes.

Remove pizza from the oven and transfer it to a cutting board. Cut into slices and enjoy immediately.

WINE PAIRING: Cakebread Cellars' Napa Valley Merlot

Spicy Shrimp

MAKES: ONE 10-INCH PIZZA

There's something really fun about shrimp on pizza. I can't really explain it, but maybe it's that it's not a typical pizza topping. Obviously, I love things that aren't typical. This one is a favorite because it uses my Pistachio Chimichurri (see page 53) and my Roasted Cherry Tomatoes (see page 80)—so it's pretty much a flavor explosion that I'm sure you'll love.

This recipe involves a bit of time management. I recommend making the Chimichurri one day in advance and making the Roasted Cherry Tomatoes while your oven is preheating.

---

1 ball dough of your choice, at room temperature

3 tablespoons Pistachio Chimichurri (page 53), divided

1 recipe Roasted Tomato Margarita (page 80)

½ jalapeño, seeded and sliced into rounds

1 cup low-moisture part-skim shredded mozzarella cheese (4 ounces)

4 ounces medium shrimp, peeled, deveined and halved lengthwise

⅛ teaspoon kosher salt

⅛ teaspoon black pepper

1 tablespoon finely chopped fresh cilantro

Place pizza stone on lowest rack in the oven or, if using a steel, place on the highest rack. Preheat oven to 500°F at least 45 minutes to 1 hour before baking.

Sprinkle a bit of fine cornmeal and all-purpose flour on a pizza peel or piece of parchment. Stretch out the dough and shape into a circle (see page 22), then transfer to prepared peel or parchment. Cover the dough with 2 tablespoons Chimichurri leaving a 1-inch border around the edge, then top with roasted tomatoes, jalapeño and cheese. Add shrimp and sprinkle with salt and black pepper.

Bake until the cheese is melted, shrimp are cooked and crust is golden, 8–10 minutes.

Remove the pizza from the oven and transfer it to a cutting board. Garnish with cilantro and drizzle top with the remaining tablespoon of Chimichurri. Cut into slices and enjoy immediately.

INGREDIENT NOTE: Buying shrimp can be confusing, but remember, in the U.S., shrimp are sold by the number per pound. Medium or large shrimp work well for this pizza, which are usually labeled, 41/50 for medium and 31/35 for large.

BRIGHT IDEA: Frozen shrimp can be used for this recipe, just thaw thoroughly and pat dry before using.

WINE PAIRING: Cannonball's Sauvignon Blanc

Prosciutto, Olives & Red Onion

MAKES: ONE 10-INCH PIZZA

I'm so happy that prosciutto and other cured meats have become more mainstream than in the past. There are a variety of fun ones to try. While I love prosciutto for this pizza, feel free to experiment with other cured meats that you find at your grocery or meat market. Speck, pancetta and capicola are all delicious options, and if all else fails, bacon is awesome too!

---

1 ball dough of your choice, at room temperature

2 tablespoons pesto or Homemade Pizza Sauce (page 45)

10 pitted green olives, roughly chopped

¼ cup thinly sliced red onion

2 ounces gouda cheese, shredded

2 ounces fresh mozzarella, sliced

1 ounce thinly sliced prosciutto

⅛ teaspoon black pepper

Place pizza stone on lowest rack in the oven or, if using a steel, place on the highest rack. Preheat oven to 500°F at least 45 minutes to 1 hour before baking.

Sprinkle a bit of fine cornmeal and all-purpose flour on a pizza peel or piece of parchment. Stretch out the dough and shape into a circle (see page 22), then transfer to prepared peel or parchment. Spread pizza sauce over dough leaving a 1-inch border around the edge, then top with olives, tomatoes, gouda and mozzarella cheeses. Lay pieces of prosciutto on top.

Bake until the cheese is melted and the crust is golden, 8–10 minutes.

Remove the pizza from the oven and transfer it to a cutting board. Garnish with black pepper. Cut into and enjoy immediately.

WINE PAIRING: Cakebread Cellars' Two Creeks Pinot Noir

Mushroom & (Some) Sausage

MAKES: ONE 10-INCH PIZZA

I am the ONLY person in my little family who likes mushrooms. If I had my way, I'd put mushrooms in everything. Since that's not happening, I find other ways to work mushrooms into dishes. One way I do that is by chopping the mushrooms up into tiny pieces. This trick magically increases overall acceptance, and because by chopping them, you get a little taste of mushroom in every bite. YUM!

Any blend of mushrooms will work for this pizza. I love the combination of cremini (also known as white or button) and shiitakes, but swap in your favorites.

---

1 tablespoon butter

1 cup roughly chopped mushrooms (button, cremini or any combination of your choice)

⅛ teaspoon kosher salt

⅛ teaspoon black pepper, plus extra for garnishing

1 ball dough of your choice, at room temperature

2 tablespoons Homemade Pizza Sauce (page 45)

¼ cup sliced black olives, drained

½ cup shredded fontina cheese (2 ounces)

½ cup shredded mozzarella cheese (2 ounces)

2 ounces bulk Italian sausage

½ cup fresh basil leaves, torn

Place pizza stone on lowest rack in the oven or, if using a steel, place on the highest rack. Preheat oven to 500°F at least 45 minutes to 1 hour before baking.

Melt the butter in a skillet set over medium high heat. Add the mushrooms, salt and black pepper, and cook, stirring, until golden brown, about 5 minutes.

Sprinkle a bit of fine cornmeal and all-purpose flour on a pizza peel or piece of parchment. Stretch out the dough and shape into a circle (see page 22). Transfer to prepared peel or parchment. Spread pizza sauce over dough leaving a 1-inch border around the edge, then top with black olives and mushrooms. Sprinkle fontina and mozzarella cheese over the top. Pinch sausage into pieces and place on top of cheese.

Bake until the cheese is melted, sausage is cooked, and crust is golden, 8–10 minutes.

Remove the pizza from the oven and transfer it to a cutting board. Garnish with black pepper and basil. Cut into slices and enjoy immediately.

WINE PAIRING: Melville Anna's Block Pinot Noir and Bread & Butter California Pinot Noir

Chorizo & Corn

MAKES: ONE 10-INCH PIZZA

If you haven't had the pleasure of trying chorizo, now is your chance. This spicy sausage used in Spanish and Mexican cooking is beyond tasty and is glorious on pizza! For this recipe, you cook and crumble it like you would with any other sausage, before adding it to your pizza. I recommend cooking up a little extra and saving it to use for tacos the next day. You'll thank me.

---

1 teaspoon vegetable or canola oil

¼ pound fresh chorizo, casings removed

1 ball dough of your choice, at room temperature

2 tablespoons Homemade Pizza Sauce (page 45)

¼ cup fresh sweet corn kernels

¼ cup finely chopped white onion

¼ cup finely chopped red bell pepper

1 cup shredded Mexican cheese blend (4 ounces)

¼ cup crumbled feta cheese or queso fresco

¼ cup chopped fresh cilantro

Hot sauce or chili oil, to taste

Place pizza stone on lowest rack in the oven or, if using a steel, place on the highest rack. Preheat oven to 500°F at least 45 minutes to 1 hour before baking.

Heat the oil in a small skillet over medium heat. Add chorizo and cook, stirring to crumble, until browned and crispy, about 10–12 minutes. Set aside.

Sprinkle a bit of fine cornmeal and all-purpose flour on a pizza peel or piece of parchment. Stretch out the dough and shape into a circle (see page 22), then transfer to prepared peel or parchment. Spread pizza sauce over dough leaving a 1-inch border around the edge, then top with cooked chorizo, corn, onion, and bell pepper. Sprinkle Mexican cheese blend and queso fresco on top.

Bake until the cheese is melted and the crust is golden, 8–10 minutes.

Remove pizza from the oven and transfer it to a cutting board. Garnish with parsley. Cut into slices and enjoy immediately. Serve with hot sauce or chili sauce, if desired.

INGREDIENT NOTE: Frozen, thawed corn can be used in place of fresh corn.

BBQ Chicken

MAKES: ONE 10-INCH PIZZA

Is this pizza super original? Perhaps not, but it's one of my favorites. I think the first version I had was at a well-known pizza chain restaurant back in the 90s. I'm pretty sure my dad ordered it and when it came to the table, I thought, "Gross, BBQ sauce on a pizza?" Ha! But of course I tried it and loved it! So here you go, this is my version of BBQ Chicken Pizza. Seeding the tomatoes may seem like an unnecessary step, but for this recipe, I think it's worth it. Removing the seeds prevents excessive liquid from pooling while the pizza cooks. This ensures a crisp crust, because soggy pizza isn't awesome.

---

1 cup shredded rotisserie or other cooked chicken

¼ cup **Easy BBQ Sauce (page 57)**, divided

1 ball dough of your choice, at room temperature

½ cup seeded, diced tomatoes

¼ cup thinly sliced red onion

¼ cup jarred sliced pepperoncini peppers

½ cup low-moisture part-skim shredded mozzarella cheese (2 ounces)

½ cup shredded gouda cheese

¼ cup roughly chopped fresh cilantro

Place pizza stone on lowest rack in the oven or, if using a steel, place on the highest rack. Preheat oven to 500°F at least 45 minutes to 1 hour before baking.

Toss the chicken with 2 tablespoons of BBQ sauce. Set aside.

Sprinkle a bit of fine cornmeal and all-purpose flour on a pizza peel or piece of parchment. Stretch out the dough and shape into a circle (see page 22), then transfer to prepared peel or parchment. Spread the remaining 2 tablespoons BBQ sauce over the dough leaving a 1-inch border around the edge, then top with chicken, tomatoes, red onion, and pepperoncini peppers. Sprinkle mozzarella and gouda cheese on top.

Bake until the cheese is melted and the crust is golden, 8–10 minutes.

Remove the pizza from the oven and transfer it to a cutting board. Garnish with cilantro. Cut into slices and enjoy immediately.

Ras El Hanout

MAKES: ONE 10-INCH PIZZA

This is definitely not a normal pizza, but I love the flavors found in North African cuisine and I wanted to make a pizza using them. It's not going to taste like a normal pizza, but that's okay. I recommend this one if you're feeling adventurous!

Room temperature hummus is easier to spread onto pizza dough than cold hummus. You can also thin it with a bit of water or lemon juice to make spreading easier.

½ cup fresh parsley

1 clove garlic

1 teaspoon lemon zest plus 2 tablespoons fresh lemon juice (from 1 lemon), divided

¼ cup plus 2 tablespoons plain Greek yogurt

2 teaspoons vegetable or canola oil

¼ pound ground lamb (or ground sirloin)

1 tablespoon tomato paste

2 teaspoons harissa seasoning (or ras el hanout spice blend)

¼ teaspoon kosher salt

1 ball dough of your choice, at room temperature

2 tablespoons **Hummus (page 58)**, room temperature

¼ cup thinly sliced red onion

¼ cup crumbled feta cheese

Place pizza stone on lowest rack in the oven or, if using a steel, place on the highest rack. Preheat oven to 500°F at least 45 minutes to 1 hour before baking.

Add the parsley, garlic, lemon zest, 1 tablespoon lemon juice, 1 tablespoon water and Greek yogurt to a blender or small food processor and blend until smooth. Transfer to a bowl. Cover and refrigerate until ready to serve pizza.

Heat the oil in a small skillet over medium heat. Add lamb and cook, stirring to crumble, until browned, about 5 minutes. Add the remaining teaspoon oil and the tomato paste and cook until color changes from bright red to brick red, 3 minutes. Stir in harissa and salt, and cook stirring constantly for 1 minute. Remove from heat, stir in remaining 1 tablespoon lemon juice and set aside.

Sprinkle a bit of fine cornmeal and all-purpose flour on a pizza peel or piece of parchment. Stretch out the dough and shape into a circle (see page 22), then transfer to prepared peel or parchment. Spread the hummus over the dough leaving a 1-inch border around the edge, then top with lamb and onion. Sprinkle feta cheese on top.

Bake until the crust is golden, 6–8 minutes.

Remove pizza from the oven and transfer it to a cutting board. Drizzle with sauce, then cut into slices and enjoy immediately.

Chicken Giardiniera

MAKES: ONE 10-INCH PIZZA

Chicagoans love giardiniera. I had no idea what it was until I moved here, but now it's a condiment we always have stocked in our refrigerator. If you can't get your hands on some, swap it with another spicy condiment of your choice. Even chopped spicy pickles will work!

1 ball dough of your choice, at room temperature

2 tablespoons Spicy Pizza Sauce (page 45)

¼ cup thinly sliced red onions

¼ cup thinly sliced red bell pepper

⅓ cup pepperoni, thinly sliced (1 ounce)

½ cup shredded rotisserie or other cooked chicken, such as my 3-Ingredient Slow Cooker Chicken (page 174)

2 tablespoons prepared giardiniera

1 cup low-moisture part-skim shredded mozzarella cheese (4 ounces)

Black pepper, for garnishing

Place pizza stone on lowest rack in the oven or, if using a steel, place on the highest rack. Preheat oven to 500°F at least 45 minutes to 1 hour before baking.

Sprinkle a bit of fine cornmeal and all-purpose flour on a pizza peel or piece of parchment. Stretch out the dough and shape into a circle (see page 22), then transfer to prepared peel or parchment. Spread pizza sauce over dough leaving a 1-inch border around the edge, then top with red onions, bell pepper, pepperoni, chicken and giardiniera. Sprinkle cheese on top.

Bake until the cheese is melted and the crust is golden, 8–10 minutes.

Remove the pizza from the oven and transfer it to a cutting board. Garnish with black pepper, cut into slices and enjoy immediately.

Breakfast Pizza

MAKES: ONE 10-INCH PIZZA

If you haven't experienced the joy of cracking an egg and putting it on pizza, well, now's your chance. Not only is the process fun, but eating it is even more fun! So, go grab your eggs and get ready for a serious treat!

---

1 ball dough of your choice, at room temperature

2 tablespoons Homemade Pizza Sauce (page 45)

1 small jalapeño pepper, thinly sliced

¼ cup diced green bell pepper

¼ cup diced red bell pepper

2 strips cooked bacon, crumbled

½ cup shredded cheddar cheese (2 ounces)

½ cup shredded mozzarella (2 ounces)

4 large eggs

⅛ teaspoon kosher salt

⅛ teaspoon black pepper

1 tablespoon finely chopped chives

Hot sauce, for serving

Place pizza stone on lowest rack in the oven or, if using a steel, place on the highest rack. Preheat oven to 500°F at least 45 minutes to 1 hour before baking.

Sprinkle a bit of fine cornmeal and all-purpose flour on a pizza peel or piece of parchment. Stretch out the dough and shape into a circle (see page 22), then transfer to prepared peel or parchment. Spread pizza sauce over dough leaving a 1-inch border around the edge, then top with jalapeño, bell peppers and bacon. Sprinkle cheddar and mozzarella cheese on top. Bake for 5 minutes.

Remove pizza from oven and make four indentations on the top using the back of a spoon. Crack eggs, one at a time, into each indentation. Season eggs with salt and black pepper. Return pizza to oven and bake until cheese is melted, egg whites are set, and crust is golden, 4–5 minutes.

Remove the pizza from the oven and transfer it to a cutting board. Garnish with chives and hot sauce, if using. Cut into slices and enjoy immediately.

METHOD TIP: Not great at cracking eggs? Crack them one at a time into a bowl, then pour onto pizza. This will make it easier to fish out any shells.

INGREDIENT NOTE: If spicy isn't what you're after, remove the seeds and membranes first, then dice instead of slicing.

Pulled Pork & Cabbage Slaw

MAKES: ONE 10-INCH PIZZA

You know you love a good pulled pork sandwich. It also makes for a great pizza! Cook the pork the day before so that you're ready to add it to your pizza the next day. Any extra can be frozen and used for other pizzas or meals.

I call for shredded coleslaw mix in this recipe because it's more convenient than chopping up a head of cabbage. It's a weekly purchase for me because I use it for tacos, salads, and everything in between. Find it in the produce section at your grocery store near packaged lettuce or salad mixes.

Note: This pizza can be heavy, I recommend making it on parchment.

1 ball dough of your choice, at room temperature

2 tablespoons Easy BBQ Sauce (page 57)

1 cup Slow-Cooker Pulled Pork (page 175)

¼ cup thinly sliced red onion

¼ cup fresh sweet corn kernels

½ cup shredded mozzarella cheese (2 ounces)

½ cup shredded cheddar cheese (2 ounces)

1 tablespoon apple cider vinegar

1 teaspoon Dijon mustard

¼ teaspoon celery seed

2 tablespoons plain Greek yogurt

¼ teaspoon kosher salt

⅛ teaspoon black pepper

½ teaspoon hot sauce, optional

2 cups shredded coleslaw mix

Place pizza stone on lowest rack in the oven or, if using a steel, place on the highest rack. Preheat oven to 500°F at least 45 minutes to 1 hour before baking.

Sprinkle a bit of fine cornmeal and all-purpose flour on a pizza peel or piece of parchment. Stretch out the dough and shape into a circle (see page 22), then transfer to prepared peel or parchment. Spread BBQ sauce over dough leaving a 1-inch border around the edge, then top with pork, red onion and corn. Sprinkle mozzarella and cheddar cheese on top.

Bake until the cheese is melted and the crust is golden, 8–10 minutes.

While pizza is cooking, make the slaw. Whisk the vinegar, mustard, celery seed, yogurt, salt, black pepper, and hot sauce together in the bottom of a large bowl. Add the slaw mix and toss to combine.

Remove pizza from the oven and transfer it to a cutting board. Top with slaw, then cut into slices and enjoy immediately.

INGREDIENT NOTE: Frozen, thawed corn can be used in place of fresh. Pat dry before use.

Baked Potato

MAKES: ONE 10-INCH PIZZA

My mom made a lot of baked potatoes for us when we were kids. I loved them and still do! This pizza tastes like a doughy baked potato! How great is that? Feel free to change up the toppings, but I love the salty crunchy bacon, cheddar cheese and fresh, chopped chives on this one! If you're having a hard time slicing your potatoes thin enough, consider using a mandolin or a food processor.

2 medium Yukon Gold potatoes, cut into ⅛-inch thick slices

2 tablespoons extra-virgin olive oil

¼ teaspoon kosher salt

⅛ teaspoon black pepper

1 ball dough of your choice, at room temperature

2 tablespoons Sara's Buttermilk Ranch (page 62), plus extra for serving

2 slices bacon, cooked and crumbled

2 tablespoons finely chopped chives, divided

1 cup shredded sharp cheddar cheese (4 ounces)

Place pizza stone on lowest rack in the oven or, if using a steel, place on the highest rack. Preheat oven to 400°F at least 45 minutes to 1 hour before baking.

Toss potatoes with oil, salt, and black pepper. Spread out in a single layer on a baking sheet lined with parchment paper. Roast, stirring once halfway through cooking, until golden and fork-tender, 25–30 minutes. Remove from oven. Increase oven temperature to 500°F.

Sprinkle a bit of fine cornmeal and all-purpose flour on a pizza peel or piece of parchment. Stretch out the dough and shape into a circle (see page 22), then transfer to prepared peel or parchment. Spread Buttermilk Ranch over dough leaving a 1-inch border around the edge, then top with potatoes, bacon and 1 tablespoon chives. Sprinkle cheese on top.

Bake until the cheese is melted and the crust is golden, 8–10 minutes.

Remove the pizza from the oven and transfer it to a cutting board. Garnish with dollops of ranch, if using, and sprinkle with the remaining 1 tablespoon chives. Cut into slices and enjoy immediately.

WINE PAIRING: Melville Estate's Syrah

Salads &
Salad-Style Pizza

147 Caesar

148 Greek

151 Cali

152 Tex Mex

154 Pac NW

155 Midwest Cobb

156 Citrus & Avocado Salad

158 Big Green Salad

159 Corn & Tomato Salad

161 Apples, Cherries & Baby Greens Salad

162 Lemony-Kale Salad

Caesar

MAKES: ONE 10-INCH PIZZA

I'm a huge fan of Caesar salads. I love the traditional variety made with egg, but I don't often make them. Instead, I channel those same ingredients and turn them into a creamy version that I think is just as delicious. Big shards of freshly shaved Parmesan are a MUST here.

---

1 ball dough of your choice, at room temperature

1 tablespoon extra-virgin olive oil

1 cup low-moisture part-skim shredded mozzarella cheese (4 ounces)

½ teaspoon Dijon mustard

1 tablespoon lemon juice (from 1 lemon)

1 clove garlic, smashed and minced

1 anchovy, finely minced (or 1 tablespoon anchovy paste)

2 tablespoons plain Greek yogurt

¼ teaspoon kosher salt

¼ teaspoon black pepper

2 tablespoons grated Parmesan cheese plus ½ cup shaved, divided

2 cups chopped romaine lettuce

1 cup grape tomatoes, sliced lengthwise

Place pizza stone on lowest rack in the oven or, if using a steel, place on the highest rack. Preheat oven to 500°F at least 45 minutes to 1 hour before baking.

Sprinkle a bit of fine cornmeal and all-purpose flour on a pizza peel or piece of parchment. Stretch out the dough and shape into a circle (see page 22), then transfer to prepared peel or parchment. Spread oil over the dough, then sprinkle mozzarella cheese on top.

Bake until the cheese is melted and the crust is golden, 8–10 minutes.

Meanwhile, make the salad. Whisk the mustard, lemon juice, garlic, anchovy, yogurt, salt, black pepper and 2 tablespoons grated Parmesan cheese together in a large bowl. Add lettuce and tomatoes and toss to combine.

Remove pizza from the oven, arrange the salad on top, garnish with remaining ½ cup shaved Parmesan cheese, then cut into slices and serve.

WINE PAIRING: Melville Estate's Chardonnay

Greek

MAKES: ONE 10-INCH PIZZA

Greek salad is an all-time favorite of mine. In Indy, there was a great Greek restaurant that made a fabulous, authentic Greek salad with giant cubes of feta and super-delicious kalamata olives. I loved it! This pizza is a celebration of those flavors!

1 ball dough of your choice, at room temperature

2 tablespoons extra-virgin olive oil, divided

1 cup low-moisture part-skim shredded mozzarella cheese (4 ounces)

½ teaspoon Dijon mustard

1 tablespoon red wine vinegar

1 teaspoon dried oregano or Italian seasoning

¼ teaspoon kosher salt

⅛ teaspoon black pepper

2 cups chopped romaine lettuce

½ cup diced bell pepper (red, orange or yellow)

½ cup diced cucumber

½ cup grape tomatoes, halved

10 pitted kalamata olives

¼ cup crumbled feta cheese

Place pizza stone on lowest rack in the oven or, if using a steel, place on the highest rack. Preheat oven to 500°F at least 45 minutes to 1 hour before baking.

Sprinkle a bit of fine cornmeal and all-purpose flour on a pizza peel or piece of parchment. Stretch out the dough and shape into a circle (see page 22). Transfer to prepared peel or parchment. Spread 1 tablespoon of oil over the dough, then sprinkle mozzarella cheese on top.

Bake until the cheese is melted and the crust is golden, 8–10 minutes.

Meanwhile, make the salad. Whisk the mustard, vinegar, Italian seasoning, salt, and black pepper together in a large bowl. Whisk in the remaining 1 tablespoon olive oil. Add lettuce, bell pepper, tomatoes, olives, and feta cheese, and toss to combine.

Remove pizza from the oven, arrange with salad on top, then cut into slices and serve.

Cali

MAKES: ONE 10-INCH PIZZA

I love California. The terrain is gorgeous and the weather is lovely. This salad is a tribute to the fabulous food that grows there!

---

1 ball dough of your choice, at room temperature

2 tablespoons extra-virgin olive oil, divided

1 cup shredded low-moisture part-skim mozzarella cheese (4 ounces)

2 teaspoons tahini

1 teaspoon lime zest and 1 tablespoon fresh lime juice (from 1 lime)

1 tablespoon rice vinegar

1 tablespoon reduced-sodium soy sauce

1 teaspoon honey

¼ teaspoon kosher salt

⅛ teaspoon black pepper

1 cup Bibb lettuce

1 ripe avocado, sliced

¼ cup sliced red onion

2 radishes, thinly sliced

½ cup shaved or thinly sliced carrot

2 tablespoons sliced almonds, toasted

Place pizza stone on lowest rack in the oven or, if using a steel, place on the highest rack. Preheat oven to 500°F at least 45 minutes to 1 hour before baking.

Sprinkle a bit of fine cornmeal and all-purpose flour on a pizza peel or piece of parchment. Stretch out the dough and shape into a circle (see page 22), then transfer to prepared peel or parchment. Spread 1 tablespoon of olive oil over the dough, then sprinkle mozzarella cheese on top.

Bake until the cheese is melted and the crust is golden, 8–10 minutes.

Meanwhile, make the salad. Whisk the tahini, lime zest, lime juice, rice vinegar, soy sauce and honey together in a large bowl. Whisk in the remaining olive oil, salt, and black pepper. Remove half and reserve. Then add lettuce, avocado, onion, radishes, carrots, and almonds to the bowl, and toss to combine.

Remove pizza from the oven, arrange with salad on top, then cut into slices and serve. Serve extra dressing on the side.

NOTE: Use a vegetable peeler to easily shave the carrots into long strands.

Tex Mex

MAKES: ONE 10-INCH PIZZA

I have been to Texas twice, and both times I was treated to some amazing Tex-Mex cuisine. If you didn't know already, I love the flavors of the Southwest and Mexico. The chiles, the beans, the fresh lime juice and avocados make for delicious food. I love using refried beans and salsa on this pizza—they make for a great base for the taco salad-like toppings.

---

1 ball dough of your choice, at room temperature

¼ cup refried beans

¼ cup **Fire-Roasted Tomato Salsa (page 61)**, divided

2 tablespoons sour cream

2 teaspoons fresh lime juice

1 cup shredded Mexican-blend cheeses (4 ounces)

2 cups chopped romaine lettuce

1 Roma tomato, seeded and diced

¼ cup thinly sliced green onion

¼ cup fresh cilantro, roughly chopped

¼ cup sliced black olives

⅛ teaspoon black pepper

¼ teaspoon kosher salt

1 ripe avocado, diced

1 tablespoon pepitas, toasted

1 cup crushed tortilla chips

Place pizza stone on lowest rack in the oven or, if using a steel, place on the highest rack. Preheat oven to 500°F at least 45 minutes to 1 hour before baking.

Sprinkle a bit of fine cornmeal and all-purpose flour on a pizza peel or piece of parchment. Stretch out the dough and shape into a circle (see page 22), then transfer to prepared peel or parchment. Spread refried beans over the dough leaving a 1-inch border around the edge, then top with 2 tablespoons salsa. Sprinkle cheese over the top.

Bake until the cheese is melted and the crust is golden, 8–10 minutes.

Meanwhile, make the salad. Whisk the remaining 2 tablespoons salsa with the sour cream and lime juice in a large bowl. Add lettuce, tomato, onion, cilantro, black olives, salt, and black pepper, and toss to combine.

Remove pizza from the oven. Arrange salad on top, and garnish with avocado, pumpkin seeds, and crushed tortilla chips. Cut into slices and serve.

Pac NW

MAKES: ONE 10-INCH PIZZA

Someday, I will live in Portland, Oregon. That's the dream. It will be in a small cottage where the biggest room in the place is the kitchen. There will be a window over the sink with a view of my garden. Sounds good, right? Until then, I'll just eat this pizza, eyes closed, envisioning my dream.

1 ball dough of your choice, at room temperature

1 tablespoon extra-virgin olive oil

1 cup low-moisture part-skim shredded mozzarella cheese (4 ounces)

¾ cup fresh blackberries, divided

1 tablespoon balsamic vinegar

⅛ teaspoon kosher salt

⅛ teaspoon black pepper

1 teaspoon honey

⅓ cup avocado oil (or any neutral-flavored oil)

2 cups mixed baby lettuces

1 shallot, thinly sliced

1 small Fuji apple, cored and sliced

¼ cup toasted hazelnuts, roughly chopped

¼ cup crumbled gorgonzola or goat cheese

Place pizza stone on lowest rack in the oven or, if using a steel, place on the highest rack. Preheat oven to 500°F at least 45 minutes to 1 hour before baking.

Sprinkle a bit of fine cornmeal and all-purpose flour on a pizza peel or piece of parchment. Stretch out the dough and shape into a circle (see page 22), then transfer to prepared peel or parchment. Spread oil over the dough, then sprinkle mozzarella cheese on top.

Bake until the cheese is melted and the crust is golden, 8–10 minutes.

Meanwhile, make the salad. Add ¼ cup blackberries, balsamic vinegar, salt, pepper, honey and oil in a blender and puree until smooth. Add lettuce, shallot and apples to a large bowl, drizzle with 2 tablespoons salad dressing and toss gently to combine. Garnish with hazelnuts, cheese and the remaining ½ cup blackberries.

Remove pizza from the oven, arrange with salad on top, then cut into slices and serve. Serve extra dressing on the side.

Midwest Cobb

MAKES: ONE 10-INCH PIZZA

The Midwest doesn't get much love, but I grew up here and I think it deserves some! While we don't have an ocean or a bunch of mountains, we have great land for growing plants and raising animals. I can't think of a salad that celebrates the Midwest more than a Cobb salad, so here's my version, on a pizza!

1 ball dough of your choice, at room temperature

1 tablespoon extra-virgin olive oil

1 cup low-moisture part-skim shredded mozzarella cheese (4 ounces)

2 tablespoons Sara's Buttermilk Ranch (page 62)

2 cups baby Boston or Bibb lettuce, torn into bite-size pieces

1 cup cherry tomatoes, halved

¼ cup thinly sliced red onion

2 hard-boiled eggs, diced

1 ounce diced ham, preferably maple-flavored

¼ cup crumbled gorgonzola cheese

1 avocado, diced

Place pizza stone on lowest rack in the oven or, if using a steel, place on the highest rack. Preheat oven to 500°F at least 45 minutes to 1 hour before baking.

Sprinkle a bit of fine cornmeal and all-purpose flour on a pizza peel or piece of parchment. Stretch out the dough and shape into a circle (see page 22), then transfer to prepared peel or parchment. Spread oil over the dough, then sprinkle mozzarella cheese on top.

Bake until the cheese is melted and the crust is golden, 8–10 minutes.

Meanwhile, make the salad. Add the lettuce, tomatoes, onion, eggs, ham, cheese, and avocado to a large mixing bowl. Add the salad dressing and toss to combine.

Remove pizza from the oven and arrange the salad on top. Cut into slices and serve immediately.

Citrus & Avocado Salad

MAKES: 4 SERVINGS

If you're looking for something bright and refreshing to pair with your pizza, this salad makes the perfect side. Feel free to segment the citrus instead of slicing, if that's easier. And before you get to zesting that fruit, make sure you wash it first!

1 large grapefruit, zested, peeled, and sliced into rounds

2 small oranges, zested, peeled, and sliced into rounds

Zest and juice from 1 lime

1 teaspoon grated fresh ginger

1 teaspoon honey

1 teaspoon Dijon mustard

2 tablespoons extra-virgin olive oil

¼ teaspoon kosher salt

⅛ teaspoon black pepper

1 head Bibb lettuce, torn into bite-size pieces

1 ripe avocado, sliced

½ cup thinly sliced red onion

¼ cup lightly salted pistachios, roughly chopped

Whisk grapefruit zest, orange zest, lime zest, 1 tablespoon lime juice, ginger, honey, and mustard in a small bowl. In a steady stream, whisk in oil. Season with salt and black pepper.

Peel the grapefruit and the oranges then slice into rounds. Arrange lettuce, avocado, and onion on a serving plate and top with sliced citrus. Drizzle dressing over everything and garnish with pistachios. Serve immediately.

Big Green Salad

MAKES: 4 SERVINGS

If a traditional side salad is what you're after, this is it. Feel free to swap ingredients based on what you have or what you like. I love red wine vinegar, but any vinegar or citrus juice would be a fine substitute. And play around with the vegetables and lettuce. It's totally customizable!

1 teaspoon Dijon mustard

2 tablespoons red wine vinegar

½ teaspoon Italian seasoning

¼ teaspoon honey

2 tablespoons extra-virgin olive oil

¼ teaspoon kosher salt

⅛ teaspoon black pepper

2 cups chopped romaine lettuce

4 cups baby spinach

1 small seedless cucumber, sliced

1 green bell pepper, thinly sliced

2 medium stalks celery, sliced on the bias

Whisk the mustard, vinegar, Italian seasoning, and honey together in a large salad bowl. Add the olive oil in a steady stream, whisking to combine. Season with salt and black pepper.

Add the romaine, spinach, cucumber, pepper, and celery and toss well with the vinaigrette.

TAKE IT UP A NOTCH: Add some crumbled gorgonzola, feta or goat cheese just before serving. Looking for some added crunch? Throw in some croutons just before serving.

INGREDIENT NOTE: If you don't have Italian seasoning, make your own! My sister-in-law (yay Marissa Haas!) kindly allowed me to share her secret recipe! To make her version simply combine the following: ⅛ teaspoon each of dried oregano, dried basil, dried thyme and dried parsley.

Corn & Tomato Salad

MAKES: 4 SERVINGS

This salad reminds me of summer. I make it all of the time when the corn is fresh and the tomatoes taste like sunshine!

2 cups fresh green beans, trimmed

1 teaspoon honey

1 teaspoon Dijon mustard

2 tablespoons fresh lime juice (from one small lime)

¼ teaspoon kosher salt

⅛ teaspoon black pepper

2 tablespoons extra-virgin olive oil

½ cup fresh cilantro, roughly chopped

1 cup fresh sweet corn kernels or thawed, frozen corn

1 pint cherry tomatoes, halved if large

¼ teaspoon kosher salt

⅛ teaspoon black pepper

¼ cup pepitas, toasted

1 ripe avocado, diced

Fill a 3 or 4-quart pot two-thirds full of water and bring to a boil over high heat. Salt the water (add 1 tablespoon kosher salt for every 2 quarts of water you use). Once boiling, add the green beans and cook for two to three minutes. Drain the green beans in a colander then run cold water over them (about 1 minute) or place in an ice bath to help stop the cooking process. Once cool to the touch, remove and pat dry with a clean towel.

Whisk the honey, mustard, lime juice, salt and black pepper together in the bottom of a large bowl. Add the olive oil in a steady stream, whisking to combine. Add the cilantro, corn, tomatoes, green beans, salt and black pepper and toss gently to combine. Refrigerate until ready to serve.

When ready to enjoy, top with pepitas and avocado and toss to combine.

PREP TIP: Salad can be made up to 1 day in advance. Store vegetables and dressing separately and add avocado just before serving.

TWIST: Want a creamy version of this salad? Whisk in 2 tablespoons of plain Greek yogurt for the oil in the dressing, then proceed with the recipe as written.

INGREDIENT OPTION: Parsley can be swapped for cilantro. And if you can't find fresh corn, swap with thawed, frozen corn.

Apples, Cherries & Baby Greens Salad

MAKES: 4 SERVINGS

Back in my 20s, I lived down the street from a really tasty pizza restaurant. They had a delicious salad on the menu that I would order at least once a week. As soon as I got home, I would eat it directly out of the plastic container and devour it like someone was going to take it away from me. It was that good. Here's my version, feel free to share, or not.

---

1 teaspoon Dijon mustard

2 teaspoons maple syrup

1 tablespoon balsamic vinegar

1 tablespoon minced shallot

¼ teaspoon kosher salt

⅛ teaspoon black pepper

2 tablespoons extra-virgin olive oil

6 cups mixed baby lettuces

¼ cup thinly sliced red onion

1 small Granny Smith apple, sliced

½ cup dried cherries

¼ cup crumbled gorgonzola or blue cheese

¼ cup toasted walnuts or pecans

Whisk the mustard, maple syrup, vinegar, shallot, salt, and black pepper together in a large salad bowl. Add the olive oil in a steady stream, whisking to combine.

Add the lettuce, onion, apple, cherries, gorgonzola, and walnuts and toss well with the vinaigrette. Serve immediately.

TOAST WALNUTS IN A SKILLET: Place walnuts in a small skillet and set over medium heat. Cook, shaking the pan frequently, until fragrant and golden, about 4–5 minutes. Remove from heat and allow to cool before adding to salad.

TOAST WALNUTS IN THE OVEN: Preheat oven to 375°F. Line a small baking sheet with foil or parchment paper. Add walnuts and bake until fragrant and golden, about 5–8 minutes. Remove from heat and allow to cool before adding to salad.

Lemony-Kale Salad

MAKES: 4 SERVINGS

Remember when kale was the coolest? Well, I still think it's the coolest. Not only because of its amazing health benefits (there are so many!), but also because of its texture and flavor! There is something fun about kale's chewy earthiness and I love it paired with bright lemon and salty Parmesan!

---

10 cups lacinato kale, stems removed and chopped

1 teaspoon lemon zest plus 2 tablespoons lemon juice (from one lemon), divided

2 tablespoons extra-virgin olive oil, divided

⅛ teaspoon kosher salt

1 tablespoon tahini

1 clove garlic, finely minced

½ cup freshly shaved Parmesan cheese

2 cups whole grain or homemade croutons

¼ teaspoon black pepper

Crushed red pepper, to taste

Add kale to a large salad bowl along with the lemon zest, 1 tablespoon lemon juice and 1 tablespoon olive oil. Massage the lemon and oil into the leaves using clean hands, for about 2 minutes. Add the salt and toss to coat. Set aside.

Whisk the tahini, garlic, 1 tablespoon lemon juice, and 1 tablespoon oil together in a small bowl.

Pour the dressing over the kale and toss to combine. Add the croutons, black pepper and a pinch of crushed red pepper and toss again. Serve immediately.

To Make Croutons

Preheat oven to 300°F. Slice bread (preferably a crusty bread such as sourdough, French bread, or a yummy whole grain boule, but any bread will do, especially one that's a little old.) into ¾ inch cubes. You should have about 2½ to 3 cups. Spread bread cubes out on a large, rimmed baking sheet lined with parchment paper and bake for 10 minutes. Remove from oven. Sprinkle with ¼ teaspoon kosher salt and ⅛ teaspoon freshly cracked black pepper (and whatever dried herbs or spices you like). Drizzle with 2 tablespoons olive oil and using clean hands, toss to coat. Return to oven and bake until crunchy and golden, about 15–20 minutes. Remove from oven and cool on a rack.

INGREDIENT NOTE: If you can't find lacinato kale, don't stress! You can use curly kale here too! It's an equal swap.

INGREDIENT NOTE: Add a few cups of baby lettuce or other greens to the salad if a bowl full of kale is too hearty for your tastes.

Dessert Pizza

166 Skillet Brownie with Chocolate
Ganache & Toasted Coconut

168 Brown-Butter Chocolate Chip
Pizza Cookie

170 Classic Fruit Pizza

171 Cinnamon-Sugar Pizza

Skillet Brownie with Chocolate Ganache & Toasted Coconut

MAKES: 12 SERVINGS

I hadn't originally planned to add a brownie recipe to this book, but thankfully, I came to my senses. Brownies happen to be my favorite dessert. Maybe it's because I love chocolate or maybe it's because I love how easy they are to make. Either way, this recipe is a new favorite around my house.

---

8 tablespoons (113 grams) unsalted butter

¾ cup (64 grams) unsweetened cocoa powder

¾ teaspoon baking powder

¼ teaspoon kosher salt

¾ cup (150 grams) granulated sugar

¼ cup (55 grams) packed light brown sugar

1 teaspoon pure vanilla extract

2 tablespoons strong coffee, cold brew coffee or espresso

2 large eggs

½ cup (60 grams) all-purpose flour

1 cup (240 grams) semisweet chocolate chips, divided

½ cup (120 grams) heavy cream

⅓ cup coconut flakes, toasted (see Note)

Sea salt, for garnish

Position rack in middle of oven and preheat to 350°F. Coat bottom and sides of a 10-inch cast iron skillet with 1 tablespoon softened butter.

Melt the remaining 7 tablespoons butter in a small saucepan over medium heat. Remove from heat and transfer to a medium mixing bowl. Cool slightly, about 5 minutes, then stir in the cocoa powder, baking powder, salt, granulated sugar, brown sugar, vanilla extract, and coffee.

Add eggs one at a time, mixing well after each addition. Fold in the flour, mixing until just combined. Stir in ½ cup chocolate chips. Scrape batter into the prepared skillet and spread out in an even layer. Bake for 25–30 minutes or until a toothpick inserted into the center comes out clean. Cool in pan on a wire rack.

While the brownie cools, make ganache. Place the remaining ½ cup of chocolate chips in a small bowl. Add the cream to a small saucepan and set over medium heat. Once cream begins to simmer, remove from heat, and pour over chocolate chips. Let sit for one minute, then slowly begin to whisk, stirring until smooth. Let the ganache cool to room temperature before glazing brownie.

Pour glaze over brownie, using a knife or off-set spatula to fully cover the top. Garnish with toasted coconut and sea salt.

NOTE: To toast coconut: Spread coconut out in an even layer on a rimmed baking sheet. Bake at 350°F until golden, stirring occasionally, 8–10 minutes.

NOTE: Butter can be melted in a large, microwave-safe bowl. Start by putting it in the microwave for 1 minute at 50 percent power, stir and return to microwave, cooking at 30 second increments at 50 percent power until melted. Allow it to cool slightly, then continue with the recipe as written.

NOTE: You can use a 12-inch cast iron skillet, but the brownies will cook faster, so check on them after 15 minutes of baking and then check every 5 minutes to see if done.

Brown-Butter Chocolate Chip Pizza Cookie

SERVINGS: 12

If you like cookies, then you'll love this cookie pizza. The browned butter is worth the extra time. It adds a rich, caramel flavor to this cookie dough that can't be beat. You can enjoy a slice as is, but it's especially good when topped with vanilla ice cream and hot fudge. Just saying.

---

11 tablespoons unsalted butter, at room temperature, divided

1⅓ cup (160 grams) all-purpose flour

½ teaspoon baking soda

½ teaspoon kosher salt

⅓ cup (67 grams) packed light brown sugar

¼ cup (50 grams) granulated sugar

1 large egg

1 teaspoon pure vanilla extract

1 tablespoon (14 grams) water

½ cup toasted chopped pecans

1 cup (170 grams) dark or semi-sweet chocolate chips

Special equipment: 10-inch cast iron skillet

Set a heat-proof bowl near the stove. (You'll be using it for your browned butter.)

Cut 10 tablespoons of butter into cubes, then add to a light-colored skillet set over medium heat, stirring constantly. Butter will begin to foam; keep stirring, adjusting heat as needed to prevent butter from rising out of the skillet. Cook and stir until butter turns from light yellow to golden brown, about 5–8 minutes. Remove from heat and pour immediately into heat-proof bowl. Set aside to cool to room temperature. (To speed up the cooling process, place butter in the refrigerator or set in an ice bath. It's okay if butter solidifies but is still soft.)

While butter cools, combine the flour, baking soda and salt together in a medium bowl. Set aside.

Preheat oven to 375°F and place one rack in the middle position in oven. Coat bottom and sides of a 10-inch cast iron skillet with remaining 1 tablespoon softened butter.

Make the cookie batter: With electric or stand mixer, beat the cooled butter with brown sugar and granulated sugar until creamy, about 3 minutes. Scrape down the sides of the bowl. Add egg, vanilla extract and water and beat to combine. Gradually add flour mixture on low speed and mix until just combined. Stir in pecans and chocolate chips. Scrape the batter into the prepared skillet and use a spatula to spread and push it out evenly into the pan. Bake until the top and sides are lightly browned and golden, about 18–20 minutes.

Remove from the oven and cool 15 minutes before slicing.

EQUIPMENT NOTE: The light-colored skillet makes it possible to see when the butter changes color. If you use a darkly-coated skillet, it'll be difficult to know when the butter has turned from light yellow to golden brown.

RECIPE NOTE: If you don't want to make the browned butter, that's A-OK! Skip that step and just use 8 tablespoons of room temperature butter for the dough (and 1 tablespoon to coat the pan) and proceed with the recipe starting with the "Preheat the oven" step.

Classic Fruit Pizza

MAKES: 8 SERVINGS

Remember this childhood favorite? I have memories of this dessert showing up at plenty of birthday parties as a kid. I suppose it was a handy dessert for the parent who didn't really feel like baking. I've included it here for my husband because when I asked him what kind of dessert pizza I should put in this book, his immediate answer was "fruit pizza." Cute, right?

Cookie Dough

1¼ cups (150 grams) all-purpose flour plus extra for rolling

½ teaspoon baking powder

¼ teaspoon kosher salt

5 tablespoons unsalted butter, softened

⅓ cup (67 grams) granulated sugar

1 large egg

¼ teaspoon pure vanilla extract

Topping

4 ounces cream cheese, softened

2 tablespoons unsalted butter, softened

1½ cups (170 grams) powdered sugar, divided

1 teaspoon orange zest (or any citrus zest)

½ teaspoon pure vanilla extract

Topping options: blueberries, blackberries, kiwi, mandarin orange slices, raspberries, strawberries

Preheat the oven to 350°F.

To prepare cookie dough: Whisk together the flour, baking powder and salt in a medium mixing bowl.

Beat the butter and sugar together in a large mixing bowl or in the bowl of a stand mixer until creamy, about 1 minute. Scrape down the sides of the bowl and add the egg and vanilla; beat until just combined. Add the flour mixture and beat on low speed until just incorporated. Shape dough into a flat disc, wrap in plastic wrap, and refrigerate for 30 minutes.

Lightly flour your work surface. Roll dough out into either a 10-inch circle or an 8x10-inch rectangle. Transfer dough to a parchment-lined baking sheet. Bake until lightly golden, 12–15 minutes. Transfer to a rack to cool.

Make the topping: Beat the cream cheese and butter together in a large bowl until light and combined, Add half of the powdered sugar and beat well. Add remaining sugar, orange zest and vanilla and beat until smooth. Spread over the cooled cookie. Top with fresh fruit, slice and serve.

STORAGE NOTE: Cookie and topping can be made up to one day in advance. Wrap the cookie in plastic wrap and store at room temperature. Refrigerate topping in a sealed container. Remove topping about 1 hour before serving to take the chill off and make it spreadable.

Cinnamon-Sugar Pizza

MAKES: 8 SERVINGS

There's nothing fancy about this cinnamon-sugar pizza, but maybe that's what makes it so delicious. Because warm dough topped with butter, cinnamon, sugar, and a little icing is always a good idea.

1 ball dough of your choice, at room temperature at room temperature

Fine cornmeal, as needed

All-purpose flour, as needed

Topping

2 tablespoons (30 grams) unsalted butter, softened

3 tablespoons packed brown sugar

2 teaspoons ground cinnamon

¼ teaspoon kosher salt

Icing

2 tablespoons (30 grams) cream cheese, softened

2 tablespoons (30 grams) unsalted butter, softened

½ teaspoon vanilla extract

1 cup (114 grams) powdered sugar

1–2 tablespoons milk

Prep dough. If refrigerated, remove at least 45–60 minutes before making pizza. Place pizza stone on lowest rack in the oven or, if using a steel, place on the highest rack. Preheat oven to 450°F at least 45 minutes to 1 hour before baking.

Sprinkle a bit of fine cornmeal and all-purpose flour on a pizza peel or piece of parchment. Stretch out the dough and shape into a circle (see page 22). Transfer to prepared peel or parchment.

Combine the butter, brown sugar, cinnamon and salt together in a small bowl until combined. Spread over the dough. Bake until crust is golden, 8–10 minutes.

While pizza is baking, make the icing. Beat the cream cheese, butter, vanilla, powdered sugar and 1 tablespoon milk together in a small bowl until combined. Thin with extra milk as needed to create a drizzling consistency.

Cut pizza into slices, then drizzle with cream cheese icing.

Perfect Pizza Extras

174 3-Ingredient Slow Cooker Chicken

175 Slow-Cooker Pulled Pork

176 Balsamic Reduction

177 Basil Goat Cheese

3-Ingredient Slow Cooker Chicken

MAKES: 8 SERVINGS

For those days when getting dinner on the table fast is a priority, you need recipes like this slow cooker chicken! Use it in tacos, on top of a salad or added to soup. It's also a great addition to pizza, go figure.

1½ pounds boneless, skinless chicken breast

¼ cup salt-free taco seasoning (or any other salt-free spice blend)

¼ cup orange juice

Place chicken in a 5–6 quart slow cooker. Rub seasoning over chicken to cover all sides. Pour orange juice around (not on top of) the chicken. Cover with a lid and cook on high for 3 hours or on low for 6 hours.

Remove the lid and pull chicken apart with two forks. Season to taste with salt.

INGREDIENT NOTE: Try a combination of boneless, skinless chicken breasts and thighs for more flavor.

STORAGE NOTE: This pulled chicken freezes well. If you don't use it all within three days, transfer it to a resealable freezer bag and use within 4 months.

Slow-Cooker Pulled Pork

MAKES: 8 SERVINGS

I love the versatility of this slow cooker pork. Of course it's awesome on pizza, but like my slow cooker chicken, you can use it just about anywhere. It's delicious in quesadillas and wraps and is a great addition to savory breakfast bowls!

2–2½ pound boneless pork loin roast

1 teaspoon kosher salt

1 tablespoon chili powder

1 teaspoon ground cumin

1 teaspoon garlic powder

½ teaspoon black pepper

1 packed tablespoon brown sugar

6 fluid ounces porter or brown ale

BBQ sauce, for serving

Place pork loin roast in a 5–6-quart slow cooker. Combine the salt, chili powder, cumin, garlic powder, black pepper, and brown sugar in a bowl. Rub mixture over all sides of the roast. Pour beer around (not on top) of the roast. Cover with a lid and cook on low for 8 hours.

Remove lid and shred (or chop) pork. Serve with BBQ sauce, if desired.

INGREDIENT NOTE: If possible, select a roast that has a good amount of "dark" (it'll have a pink hue to it) meat on it. The white meat (lighter in color on the roast) is leaner and won't shred as nicely as the darker meat. If you can't find one, boneless pork shoulder is a great substitute.

INGREDIENT SWAP: If you don't want to use beer for this recipe, substitute with an equal amount of chicken broth. For a little extra flavor, stir in 1 tablespoon molasses, if you have it.

STORAGE NOTE: This pulled pork freezes well. If you don't use it all within three days, transfer it to a resealable freezer bag and use within 4 months.

Balsamic Reduction

MAKES: ABOUT ¼ CUP

Balsamic reduction was a big deal a while back. I think we overdid it a bit then, but I'm resurrecting it! It's such a simple ingredient that adds a touch of sweet, tangy goodness. It's delicious on so many things, including pizza, but also salads, sandwiches and even drizzled over soup!

½ cup balsamic vinegar

Place balsamic vinegar in a small saucepan and bring to a boil over medium heat. Reduce heat to a simmer; cook for 10 minutes or until reduced by half. Vinegar is done when it's thick enough to coat the back of a spoon. Set aside to cool. Cover and refrigerate and use within five days.

Basil Goat Cheese

MAKES: ABOUT ¼ CUP

I stumbled upon this recipe when I looked in my fridge and decided to play with the ingredients I had in there. The goat cheese came first and then I thought, "Hmm, that basil would be yummy mixed with that." Then came the garlic, salt, and black pepper and that was it. I use a small food processor to blend everything, but if you don't have one, no problem, just finely chop the basil and garlic and stir to combine.

¼ cup crumbled goat cheese, room temperature

1 cup fresh basil

2 cloves garlic

1 tablespoon milk

⅛ teaspoon kosher salt

⅛ teaspoon black pepper

Place the goat cheese, basil, garlic, milk, salt and black pepper in the bowl of a small food processor and blend, scraping down sides occasionally, until light smooth and combined.

Refrigerate and use within three days.

Interviews & Insights

AN INTERVIEW WITH WINEMAKER THOMAS VOGELE

Q: Wine is so good with pizza, why do you think that is?

A: In our opinion, it is simply because each is so enjoyable on its own and when enjoyed together, they create a perfect moment of happiness.

Q: If you could give three or four pointers for pairing wine with pizza, what would they be?

A: The wine should complement the pizza sauce and toppings. Think about how you would describe the pizza and find a wine that fits a similar description. If the pizza is light and fresh, the wine can be too. Similarly, if the pizza is bold and rich, look for those characteristics in a wine. If you aren't sure about what varietal to pick, go for a blend. But most importantly, drink a wine that you enjoy, regardless of what would be considered an appropriate pairing.

Q: Do you recommend a certain type of grape based on certain ingredients?

A: Not necessarily, although I'm sure there are experts who have honed their palates and would definitely be that specific. That feels like a very daunting assignment to us. So we say it is more about enjoyment. If you love the wine and you love the pizza, have them together. How could you go wrong with that approach?

Q: Can you provide some tips on choosing a good wine without being over-whelmed by all of the options? What can I look for to help me choose?

A: Don't be afraid to try something new. Price does not always reflect what tastes the best. Look for the reviews, scores and tasting notes that are often posted next to wine. Consider picking the wine within your price range with the highest score. It is okay to pick a wine because you like the label.

Q: Do I need to decant every bottle of wine?

A: Decanting applies to red wines and no, not every bottle needs decanting. We rarely take the time to decant a wine, but some wines will definitely taste better after they have been opened for a few hours. Decanting can be a fun part of the experience of getting to know a wine. Try the wine right after you've opened it, then again after an hour or two and maybe even the next day. It is amazing how the flavors will evolve.

Q: Does the glass shape of my wine glass really matter? Why or why not?

A: Yes, to some degree, but not enough to require you to buy new glassware. For example, if you are drinking a big bold Syrah, using a larger Bordeaux glass allows more of the wine's surface area to contact the air so the wine will "open up" (similar to what happens when a wine is decanted). But for us, it comes down to personal preference. What do you want to hold while you are drinking and what will fit through the dishwasher later?

Q: Can I drink my favorite wine with any pizza or is that a huge faux pas?

A: Absolutely, that is the enjoyment of wine—you can drink it with anything you wish (or nothing at all). Thankfully, we can all relax because the days of wine "faux pas" are long gone.

Q: Anything else you can recommend? What are your thoughts on pairing wines with veggie-forward pizzas!

A: We could probably all benefit from more veggies in our diets, so getting them onto a pizza is a great idea! We would generally recommend white or rosé wines but taking an "anything goes" approach may be more fun, so why not try a glass of bubbles!

AN INTERVIEW WITH ANDREW JANJIGIAN

Q: **Can you share any tips about how to know when dough is properly hydrated? I think this can be the hardest part of making pizza dough for a lot of people. They follow the recipe and are frustrated because they don't realize making the dough can be a bit nuanced. What should the dough look like? What should it feel like?**

First and foremost, you want to start with a good recipe, and stick with it, at least at first. Hydration is only something you need to worry about if the recipe isn't good, or no longer suits your desired results or skill level. And pizza dough doesn't *need* a lot of water to be great, though sometimes it can be desirable to use as much water as possible, as long as the dough isn't overly sticky and hard to handle.

Q: **Similarly, how do you know when you've kneaded it long enough? My old culinary school chef told us it was done when we heard the "angel wings" flapping inside the stand mixer bowl. I've always used that as my guide. :) But maybe you have some awesome visual cues to share?**

Honestly, I think people over-knead most pizza and bread doughs. Recipes often give cues for a "well" developed dough, like the windowpane test, but I never bother with those. Pizza is meant to be tender (or crisp-tender) and easy to stretch; too much kneading can make it tough or hard to stretch (where overworking it will then make it tough). As long as a dough is developed *enough*—to the point where it is even and no longer sticky—it will likely be fine.

Q: When do you like to add the salt to your dough? There are many differing opinions here; I'd love to hear yours.

I almost always use an autolyse at the start of my dough recipes. What that means is that it gets a short mix *without the salt included,* just long enough to combine the flour, water, and other ingredients fully. It then rests for about 20 minutes, during which time the flour hydrates and gluten begins to develop on its own. The salt is then added and the dough is mixed briefly, maybe 60–75 percent of the length of time that other recipes require.

Q: I like to use a bit of oil in my dough when I use whole wheat flours. Do you do this as well? If so, does it matter when you add it? Or do you just go with a straight-dough method?

I usually add oil to *all* of my pizza doughs, in 2–5 percent amounts, relative to flour weight, because it helps tenderize them.

Q: Is it better to go with an overnight fermentation in the refrigerator than a same day dough?

Almost always, because that lets the dough relax for easy stretching, while flavor develops. And I much prefer shaping the dough into balls before they go into the fridge, so that they don't need to be handled again until stretch time. (Just be sure to shape them into smooth, taut balls.)

Q: Your thoughts on placement of the baking stone and baking steel in the oven? Are you a top rack or bottom rack or other location fan? Can you explain?

I like to put mine as high in the oven as will fit comfortably, leaving 3–4 inches of space above it to easily get the pie in and out of the oven. This means either putting it onto the top rack or the next one down. That's because you want to use reflected heat from the roof of the oven to cook the top of the pie at the same rate as the bottom cooks.

Q: What's your favorite pizza topping?

Tough call, I have lots. Homemade mushroom confit, anchovies, *soppressata* and . . . hot honey.

Resources

BAKING STEEL

www.bakingsteel.com

When it comes to pizza-making, tools matter. You don't need a lot of them, but the ones you do need are important. As you already know, I can't live without my Baking Steel. If I want to replicate any good pizzeria pizza without access to a super-hot oven, I need the steel. They're also great at cooking so many other things too, like English muffins and bread!

BOOS BLOCK

www.johnboos.com

This is where I get all of my cutting boards. I met my first Boos block when I worked at Trotter's To Go. It was love at first use. I immediately went out and bought one and haven't bought anything except Boos since. Here's the deal: I love my boards, they're like family to me. I use them every day, so I want something that works and lasts. Boos boards are it. Plus, I think it's super cool that they're made in America, in Effingham, IL, which is just a hop, skip and a jump away from me. Someday I will buy myself one of their all-wood kitchen island tops.

NORDICWARE

There's something magical about a great kitchen tool and to me, baking sheets are no exception. My favorite brand of baking sheet is NordicWare. They're sturdy, come in a variety of sizes and are easy to clean.

SOUPER CUBES®

www.soupercubes.com

Souper Cubes is a small family business based in California which is passionate about making freezer meal prep easy and convenient. Their patented and innovative trays are designed to freeze food in portioned amounts.

Since I love using my freezer to help with meal prep, I love using the Souper Cubes line of silicone freezing molds. They come in a variety of sizes and are perfect for storing extra sauce, tomato paste, and anything else you're looking to freeze. My favorite is the 2 tablespoons/1 ounce tray, which I use to freeze almost every sauce in this book!

KING ARTHUR FLOUR

Flour is just flour, right? Wrong! Using high-quality flour improves your pizza dough, I promise. King Arthur Flour is the brand I choose most often for pizza dough. It's consistent and reliable.

King Arthur Flour also makes a fantastic pizza stone. Mine is durable and easy to move into and out of my oven.

BOB'S RED MILL

If I'm looking for cornmeal or specialty flours, I go for Bob's Red Mill brand. Their products are always delicious and I appreciate that they provide so much information about what's in the bag and how to use it.

WINERIES IN THIS BOOK

There are plenty of great wineries out there, but these are a few of my favorites. I definitely recommend checking them out!

Cakebread Cellars

Luke Vineyards

Melville Estates

Cannonball

Bread and Butter Wines

Acknowledgments

M Y DEEPEST THANKS AND APPRECIATION go out to:

Mike & Emily

Mom & Dad

Matt Coffman

Rick Reed

Marissa Haas

My extended family

Tom Beckman

Baking Steel

Breana Killeen

Joanie Simon

Nick Anderson

Jenny Passione

About the Author

Sara Haas, RDN, LDN, is a food and nutrition expert with formal training in the culinary arts. She works as a freelance writer, recipe developer, food photographer, media authority, public speaker and consultant dietitian/chef.

Sara is a former culinary and nutrition instructor and served as a National Academy of Nutrition and Dietetics Media Spokesperson. Sara has been featured in *Eating Well Magazine*, Allrecipes, The Kitchn, Simply Recipes, Spruce Eats, *Shape Magazine, Parents Magazine, U.S.A. Today, The Wall Street Journal, The Huffington Post* and *Epicurious*. She has previously written *Fertility Foods Cookbook* and *Taco! Taco! Taco!*

Sara shares her love of food and nutrition on her website (sarahaasmedia.com) and on Instagram (@cookinRD) and YouTube where she posts recipes, as well as nutrition and cooking tips.

Recipe Index

3-Ingredient Slow Cooker Chicken 174

A

Apples, Cherries & Baby Greens Salad 161
Asparagus, Artichoke Hearts & Capers 94
Asparagus & Pistachio 86

B

Baked Potato 143
Balsamic Reduction 176
Basil Goat Cheese 177
Basil Pesto 54
BBQ Chicken 136
BBQ Kale 99
Big Green Salad 158
Breakfast Pizza 141
Brown-Butter Chocolate Chip
    Pizza Cookie 168
Brussels Sprouts & Pecorino 107

C

Caesar 147
Cali 151
Capers, Sun-Dried Tomatoes & Basil 103
Chicken Giardiniera 139
Chorizo & Corn 135
Cinnamon-Sugar Pizza 171
Citrus & Avocado Salad 156
Classic Fruit Pizza 170
Corn & Tomato Salad 159
Crushed Tomato & Basil Sauce 46

D

Double-Dough Pan Pizza 115

E

Easy BBQ Sauce 57

F

Fire-Roasted Tomato Salsa 61

G

Giardiniera & Spinach 90
Gluten-Free Pizza Dough 40
Greek 148
Green Olive & Chimichurri 112
Grilled Pesto Chicken 122
Grilled Vegetable Pizza 72

H

Half & Half Same Day Dough 36
Harissa, Chickpeas & Cilantro 75
Homemade Pizza Sauce 45
Hominy, Poblano & Cilantro 96
Hot Hawaiian 120
Hummus 58
Hummus & Roasted Red Pepper 111
Hungry Artist 124

L

Lemon, Shaved Parmesan & Arugula 68
Lemony-Kale Salad 162

M

Midwest Cobb 155
Mushroom & (Some) Sausage 132

N

Next Day Pizza Dough 38

O

Olive & Sun-Dried Tomato Tapenade 50
Olive Tapenade 93

P

Pac NW 154
Peach & Jalapeño 100
Pepperoncini Peppers, Shredded Kale
    & Roasted Red Peppers 71
Pesto, Spinach & Basil Goat Cheese 108
Pistachio Chimichurri 53
Pistachio Chimichurri & Ricotta 104
Potato & Sausage 123
Prosciutto, Olives & Red Onion 131
Pulled Pork & Cabbage Slaw 142

R

Ras El Hanout 138
Ricotta, Balsamic Onions & Pecans 89
Roasted Mushroom & Goat Cheese 84
Roasted Red Pepper Sauce 49
Roasted Tomato Margarita 80

S

Same Day Pizza Dough 34
Sara's Buttermilk Ranch 62
Sausage, Fennel & Fontina 127
Sauteed Garlic Greens 74
Simple Margarita 79
Skillet Brownie with Chocolate Ganache &
    Toasted Coconut 166
Slow-Cooker Pulled Pork 175
Spicy Cilantro Oil 56
Spicy Shrimp 128
Spicy Southwest 67
Spinach, Hearts of Palm & Feta 83
Sun-Dried Tomato, Feta,
    Kalamata & Spinach 76

T

Tex Mex 152
Thin Crust 116